Better Homes and Gardens®

YOUR FAMILY CENTERS

BETTER HOMES AND GARDENS® BOOKS

Editor: Gerald M. Knox
Art Director: Ernest Shelton
Managing Editor: David A. Kirchner

Associate Art Director (Managing): Randall Yontz
Associate Art Directors (Creative): Linda Ford, Neoma Alt West
Copy and Production Editors: Marsha Jahns, Nancy
Nowiszewski, Mary Helen Schiltz, David A. Walsh
Assistant Art Directors: Harijs Priekulis, Tom Wegner
Graphic Designers: Mike Burns, Alisann Dixon, Mike Eagleton,
Lynda Haupert, Deb Miner, Lyne Neymeyer, Stan Sams,
D. Greg Thompson, Darla Whipple, Paul Zimmerman

Editor in Chief: Neil Kuehnl
Group Editorial Services Director: Duane L. Gregg

General Manager: Fred Stines
Director of Publishing: Robert B. Nelson
Director of Retail Marketing: Jamie Martin
Director of Direct Marketing: Arthur Heydendael

All About Your House: Your Family Centers

Project Editor: James A. Hufnagel
Associate Editor: Willa Rosenblatt Speiser
Assistant Editor: Leonore A. Levy
Contributing Senior Writer: Paul Kitzke
Copy and Production Editor: Nancy Nowiszewski
Building and Remodeling Editor: Joan McCloskey
Furnishings and Design Editor: Shirley Van Zante
Money Management and Features Editor: Margaret Daly

Art Director: Linda Ford
Graphic Designer: D. Greg Thompson

Contributors: Karol Brookhouser, James Downing,
Kim Garretson, Rose Gilbert, Cathy Howard, Jean LemMon,
Jill Mead, Stephen Mead, Jerry Reedy

Special thanks to William Hopkins, Babs Klein, and
Don Wipperman for their valuable contributions to this book.

INTRODUCTION

Your Family Centers might have been three books—Your Living Room, Your Dining Room, and Your Family Room. But as we thought about these "rooms," we came to realize that their functions overlap, and often it's difficult to draw a line where one ends and the other begins. So we've elected to combine information about all three rooms in one volume.

You can use many of the same decorating and planning elements when designing your living, dining, and family rooms. Furniture obviously plays a key role, as do efficient shelving and other built-ins. In many households, family centers are also activity centers where games, hobbies, or other special interests are enjoyed. Naturally, a wood-burning fireplace or stove offers a cozy focus for any family gathering place.

Your Family Centers covers all of these topics in detail. First you'll learn how to give dining, living, and family rooms the look you want, and how to spend your furniture dollars wisely. Are you vexed by a disorganized space? Planned projects you build can turn it into a space that really works. Your Family Centers takes you step by step through the process of planning and building storage and seating units, and offers 18 examples of furniture designs you can adapt to your needs. Outfitting rooms for fun and games, choosing the wood-burning heater that's right for you, keeping furnishings looking their best—Your Family Centers examines just about every aspect of your home's main activity areas.

Other volumes in the ALL ABOUT YOUR HOUSE series treat additional rooms or elements of a home with the same thoroughness. This important new library of books taps the experience and resources that Better Homes & Gardens. has acquired in more than 60 years of home service.

CHAPTER 6

CREATING MODULAR SEATING

The basics of furniture design
Plan the boxes

Select a finish
Build a series of boxes
How to make cushions for the finished unit

CHAPTER 7

ROOMS FOR FUN & GAMES

Video centers
Audio centers
Movies & slides
Music
Small table games

Big table games
Crafts/sewing
Wet bars
Indoor gardening
Play spaces

CHAPTER 8

KEEPING WARM WITH WOOD

Choosing a wood energy unit
Making an existing fireplace more efficient
Restyling a fireplace

Selecting a wood-burning stove
Living with a wood-heat unit

CHAPTER 9

FAMILY CENTER PROJECTS YOU CAN BUILD

Tables
Furniture by the roomful
Storage units

CHAPTER 10

CLEANING & MAINTAINING YOUR FURNISHINGS

Wood furniture
Casual furniture

Upholstery
Carpet & draperies

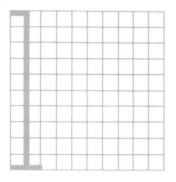

GETTING
CENTERED

Family centers are places
you go home to. They're
the spots in your house
—living room, dining room,
family room—where people
gather in a sociable setting,
ready for relaxation. In
most houses, these spaces
are interrelated: They have
common problems, often
with common solutions.
Your Family Centers is an
information-packed guide
to creating sociable living
centers for your own home.
This introductory chapter
will help you ask important
questions about your cen-
ters. When you have the
questions in mind, turn to
the chapters mentioned for
detailed answers.

WHAT ROOM DOES YOUR FAMILY LIKE BEST?

Think about it for a sec-
ond. Where your family
likes to spend time may
have little to do with the layout
of your house and more to do
with the group's habits, needs,
and interests. For example, if
family members eat together
and enjoy spending extra time
around the table talking after
dinner, then that area of the
house may be your true family
center. Chapter 2—''Recipes
for Successful Eating Spaces''
—describes a number of ways
to cook up gracious places to
dine and chat.

On the other hand, your
family may rarely eat together.
If so, the center may be an
inviting family room where
people can watch television,
play games, or enjoy a tall
cool drink before dinner.
Chapter 7—''Rooms for Fun
and Games''—contains helpful
advice on how to make such
a room come true.

Once you know where ev-
erybody likes to congregate,
take a good look at the room.
Does it accommodate the family's different interests as well
as it might? If table tennis is
popular, for instance, is your
center designed to handle the
game (see pages 110 and
111 for more information)?

The family center shown *at
right* is a room for all reasons.
Literally at the center of the
house, it's a living/dining/
kitchen area that does a number of jobs well. For example,
the person working in the
kitchen is not cut off from conversation in the rest of the
room. Yet the kitchen itself,
though part of the center, is
definitely set off from the main
living space. In addition, the
decorating theme is a wonder-
ful blend of styles. Chapter
3—''Live-in Rooms with the
Look You Want''—outlines
ideas to help you make your
family center a pleasant sight.

WHAT'S YOUR TYPICAL DAYTIME SCHEDULE?

Once you've pinpointed your family center or centers, evaluate how you use them during the daytime hours. Do toddlers head there first thing in the morning? Do they bustle with action when kids roar home after school? Are they comfortable retreats where you like to sip a late-morning cup of coffee? Or do they lie dormant throughout the day? This page and page 11 tell how the answers to these questions can shape your family centers.

Where does the day go? Live-in rooms are places where you spend most of your time. Whether it's the living room, family room, or other spot, that area should be the most congenial, most comfortable part of the house. Chapter 3—"Live-in Rooms with the Look You Want"—discusses a sensible series of ways to transform your family center into a stylishly livable room.

Of course, how and where you decorate depends on what's happening during the day. If you have young children at home, you probably want to keep an eye on them most of the time. A livable family center may be a space near the kitchen or home office.

Further, if both adults and children share the family center, it should be able to accommodate everyone. You may even want to provide access to the outside so kids don't have to ramble through the entire house to reach the family center.

In contrast, when one parent is at home, with children at school and spouse at work, the center may belong to that person for most of the day. In that case, it should be suited to the needs of the adult who's at home most.

Mother and daughter spend a lot of time together in the apartment shown *at left*. To work successfully, this room has to account for the needs of each person. It accomplishes the objective with furnishings that appeal to the mother without compromising the wishes of her daughter. In quality and appearance, they appeal to an adult's taste and sense of style. At the same time, a child can play freely here: The furnishings are not easily damaged nor are they likely to cause injury.

WHAT HAPPENS IN THE EVENINGS AND ON WEEKENDS?

Does your family center lead an active night life? If so, gauge what family members like to do—or would like to do—and see if the area measures up. Their tastes may run to relatively free-wheeling diversions: playing music, shooting pool, or smacking a table tennis ball. If their activities are real noise-makers, then a place isolated from the quiet locations in your house—perhaps a recreation room in the basement or attic—may be the best way to have fun and hold down the noise. However, if your family enjoys more tranquil pursuits, like reading or playing a serious game of cards, a retreat similar to the one *at left* may be the right spot.

Does a family center have to be in the middle of things? Not necessarily. It may be located away from the center of the house and, in certain cases, probably should be. True, an out-of-the-way location may not be a "center" as such, but it may work more efficiently, nonetheless.

The kitchen is one off-center location where your family may like to gather during the evenings and on weekends for lively conversation or late-night snacks. The rooms shown here are other working examples. Both are located in basements. The one *at left* is perfect for subdued evenings and weekends. The center *above*, in contrast, is a great place to sound off. Because the owners put some thought into selecting building materials and furnishings, neither looks as though it's underground. In the quiet room, for instance, rough-sawn cedar makes up the walls, brick pavers cover a conventional slab, and an

antique armoire conceals a television set and stereo equipment, which are standard gear in rooms like this. For more information on positioning video and stereo components, see pages 102-105.

The other room comes alive with the sound of music. To gain floor space for dancing, you can quickly disassemble the table tennis platform and store it in halves. Check pages 106 and 107 for other ideas on how to lay out a music center. To get specific information on the amount of space you need to play table tennis and other big-table games, see pages 111 and 112.

GETTING CENTERED

DO YOUR CENTERS GET RUGGED USE?

Surface materials, furnishings, and built-in storage all play key roles in the success of any activity center. If your family center is in for a rough time, make selections you can live with—materials and furniture designed to take the punishment. Choose them wisely, and you'll spend most of your days and nights enjoying the room—not repairing damage to it.

Even a group of highly active teenagers would have trouble inflicting serious damage on the room shown *at right.* The brick floor and fireplace wall are nearly indestructible, but their durability doesn't detract from the room's warm, country feeling. In fact, it adds to the decorating style, as do the heavy wood beams. Other equally durable surfaces, which may go better with the way you want your room to look, are also good choices: resilient flooring, tough indoor/outdoor carpeting, and paneling.

The wood furniture pieces are pleasantly rugged, ready to stand up to the hardest living. Similarly, the upholstered furniture is covered in easy-to-care-for fabrics, and the braided rug is not only a charming addition to the room, but is simple to clean as well.

Getting the most out of a family center means, in part, getting the most out of the things you put into it. Chapter 4—"Choosing and Buying Furniture"—is a detailed buying guide to furniture that's right for your room. If, for example, you want to fill the family center with upholstered pieces, see pages 64-66; they'll tell you how to get the best value for your money.

Chapters 5 and 6—"Creating Built-in Storage" and "Creating Modular Seating" —depict ways to organize your family center using custom units. Chapter 9—"Family Center Projects You Can Build" —offers practical ideas you can borrow and adapt to the specific requirements of your room.

And when everything's in order, check out Chapter 10— "Cleaning and Maintaining Your Furnishings"; it describes how to care for the items that you own.

WHERE DO GUESTS GATHER?

"I wonder where we go from here?" is a question most visitors ask themselves after stepping into your house. The answer they choose can tell you quite a bit about what's right—and wrong—with your family centers. If, for instance, guests are consistently attracted to a room you never thought of as a place in which to converse or entertain, maybe it's time to start viewing that area in another light. Are there improvements you can make that will allow guests to feel even more at home? On the other hand, perhaps it's a better idea to concentrate on developing a part of the house where *you* want visitors to gather.

What happens when people stop to visit? Do they drift toward the kitchen? Do you want them to? If you do, check Chapter 2—"Recipes for Successful Eating Spaces." It describes ways to make your dining area more inviting.

Of course, entertaining in the kitchen may not be your cup of tea. Solve the problem by playing up other rooms in the house. Chapter 3—"Live-in Rooms with the Look You Want"—shows how.

Your objective is to create a friendly spot where guests can relax unself-consciously and where *you* can feel comfortable entertaining them. Creating a center that plays this dual role may take some work, but, for the most part, it's a matter of analyzing your own requirements, observing the preferences of your guests, and building your solution around the two.

The people shown *at right* are obviously having a good time. The hostess is easily preparing a snack without diverting attention from her visitors, while the guests are enjoying informal hospitality without feeling they're in the way.

The key to this successful relationship is a well-placed peninsula that combines a food preparation counter with an elevated snack bar in matching butcher block. (You can buy a similar ledge ready-made and attach it in minutes with brackets and screws.) If the hostess were entertaining a larger group in the dining room, the ledge could serve as a handy buffet.

In fact, the area is a good example of how to merge two living areas—kitchen and dining room—into one cohesive whole. Pages 30 and 31 present other ways to do the same thing.

DOES YOUR HOME LACK A FAMILY ROOM?

Family rooms are probably the most popular family centers around. Yet many houses —maybe yours—don't have one. Consider the reasons why. In some homes, every inch of space is already being used for other purposes. If that's the case in your home, you'll have to make room by adding on. In others, however, owners just don't take advantage of what's there to begin with. Attics or basements go undeveloped; big formal dining rooms remain unoccupied. If you *do* have space to play with, think about turning it into the kind of family room you've always wanted.

Adding on is often an expensively impractical idea. Because putting up an addition costs more —sometimes far more—than simply incorporating the room when the house is being built, you may find the total bill too much to handle. And even if you can afford to build one, a family room may not add a great deal to the value of your house.

Don't despair, however; consider using the space you already have. Many people discover new life in old rooms, especially large, formal living rooms. By transferring a few favorite things from other parts of the house, they create full-fledged family rooms. In addition, modular furnishings, which are flexible in form and function, work well in conversions like this. (See pages 72 and 73 for advice on how to select the best in modular design, and Chapter 6—"Creating Modular Seating"—for information on planning and building a simple project.)

The family room *at right* used to be a living room. In some ways, it still is. But now it's much more. For example, the family eats at the round oak table, which expands to accommodate dinner guests. They can move the chairs away from the table to provide additional seating, if necessary. The kitchen is conveniently located to the right; you can see a storage rack peeking into the photo from behind the table. Plus, the adjustable fixtures provide different levels of light, depending on where it's needed most.

The shelves store bar utensils and a few collectibles; the little white trolley provides extra storage. Built-ins, like those described in Chapter 5— "Creating Built-in Storage"— would work equally well.

DO YOU REALLY NEED A FORMAL DINING ROOM?

Many dining rooms are perfectly decked out and beautiful to behold —yet no one pays attention to them. At a time when eating arrangements are more casual and carefree, formal dining areas simply seem too pretentious; they're not places where you can relax and enjoy a meal. Even more important, space is at a premium in many of today's smaller houses. It simply doesn't pay to have a large room go to waste. What's the answer? One idea is to convert the room you have now into a place you can use every day.

Chapter 2—"Recipes for Successful Eating Spaces"—describes a number of gracious alternatives to the traditional dining room. Here are several:
• Carefully rearrange furniture to find the space you need; see pages 24 and 25.
• Streamline your eating area. Pages 26 and 27 show how to keep things simple.
• Be flexible. Pages 28 and 29 tell you how practical furniture and accessories can create an instant dining room.
• To make a room feel larger than it is, try merging a dining area into other spots in your home; see pages 30 and 31.
• Consider dining in unlikely parts of the house. Pages 32 and 33 suggest how.
• Use the area for other activities; see pages 36 and 37 for advice on how to make a room do double-duty.

The dining room shown *at right* used to be standoffishly formal. Rarely used, its main function was to serve as a passageway between the kitchen and the rest of the house. Reincarnated, it's not only a better place to eat, but it performs a number of other functions, as well.

The owners cut a pass-through to the kitchen to facilitate service and make their clean-up chores easier. Then they furnished the room with a collection of American primitives, creating, in the process, a relaxed country look.

Each piece adds something to the aesthetic appeal of the room, yet each also has a function to perform. Antique bentwood chairs surround a Victorian oak dining table. A vintage corner cupboard contributes to the rustic charm, while also displaying several serving pieces. On the other side of the room, *below,* an antique Pennsylvania hanging cupboard and a pie safe with pierced tin doors round out the uncomplicated country theme.

DO YOU SHARE HOBBIES OR SPECIAL INTERESTS?

Planning one of your family centers to accommodate hobbies and special interests is a good idea, especially if a number of people enjoy similar things. A made-over basement or attic may be just the spot to take care of several different pursuits. Chapter 7—"Rooms for Fun & Games"—covers a variety of ways to make a family center bustle with activities, including the amount of space you need to do each. Often, too, this kind of family center requires extra storage and seating. Chapters 5 and 6 offer suggestions on how to plan and build your own.

A basement, attic, or garage is "found" space, valuable room you can use without putting up an expensive addition. Just finish it off to your liking, and you've picked up a family center for next to nothing. (See the box *at right* for additional information.)

Pages 10 and 11 show how you can take advantage of space in a basement to create two special family centers. The room *at left* is an example of how some other homeowners achieved a similar result in their attic.

The room doesn't look much like an attic, does it? Only the pitched roof gives away the disguise of the room. The rest compares favorably with most standard living rooms, although the owners deliberately chose shiplap pine for an informal look. They added plenty of insulation behind the pine, then finished off the room with wall-to-wall shag carpeting, a modular sofa, antique stove, and a drawing table for the designer in the family. The real designer isn't sitting there, but the young man helps to make a point: Just because a corner has been set up for one kind of activity doesn't mean it can't be used for others when the usual occupant isn't around.

If several people wanted to work or play up here, they might each stake out a corner. Or they could construct a long work counter to provide for everybody at once. Tools and materials could be stored in separate cabinets above and below the counter. As you see in this photograph, there's still plenty of room for others in the family to simply read, relax quietly, or talk.

SIZING UP "FOUND" SPACE

- *Attic.* This area may be at the top of your list, but ask some basic questions first. Is there enough headroom? Anything under 10 feet is probably too cramped. Think of access. If you already have a stairway with adequate headroom, getting to the top shouldn't be hard. But if you don't have any easy way up, you'll have to add a set of stairs. Will the existing floor support new living space? Contact a professional to find out.
- *Basement.* Turning a basement into a family center is often a good idea: heating, wiring, and plumbing are usually already there; space is generally ample; and access isn't a big problem. And if you don't have a lot of money to spend, you can probably do most of the work yourself.
- *Garage.* This may be the place to be. Footings, roof, and exterior walls are already in place, and most garages are close to another family center or to the kitchen. Plus, getting natural light is no problem. In addition, the architecture of the garage usually harmonizes nicely with the rest of the house. On the other hand, you may have difficulty overcoming restrictive building codes and low ceilings.

COULD GATHERING AROUND A CHEERY FIRE HELP CUT YOUR HEATING COSTS?

Few rooms are cozier than a family center with a warm, snapping fire. It's a great place to enjoy comfortable conversation and relaxing camaraderie. Using wood to warm a room (or rooms) is a charmingly traditional way to make everyone feel at home. Yet burning all that wood *efficiently* is a modern-day problem that needs to be solved before you fall too much in love with the idea.

Are you warming up to the notion of heating with wood? Chapter 8 —"Keeping Warm with Wood"— should fire your interest even further. Before you get too involved, however, see page 120; for some people in some places, it's just not a practical idea.

If you have an existing fireplace, it may be robbing your family center of heat, rather than adding warmth to it. Pages 122 and 123 explain how all that warmth can easily go up in smoke. A conventional hearth may leave you cold, but pages 124 and 125 explain how you can make it more efficient by installing a fireplace insert and by checking some basic problems common to many fireplaces and chimneys.

Once you have a fireplace heating with happy efficiency, you may decide that it's time for a change of face. Pages 126 and 127 discuss in detail how to restyle a fireplace on your own.

Other burning ideas

If you want to add one of the more modern wood-burning units available on the market, turn back to pages 122 and 123. There you'll find how to choose the best kind of unit for your house—from airtights, to heat-circulating fireplaces, to freestanding units, to relatively exotic multifuel furnaces.

Wood-burning stoves, like the two shown here, are often ideal ways to warm up a family center. The one *opposite* is a freestanding fireplace that not only contributes to the cheery, homespun atmosphere in the

room, but also puts out enough warmth to heat every square inch.

The wood stove *above* is an antique Round Oak. As you can see, it vents into a large brick fireplace on the other side of a partition separating the upper and lower halves of a divided living room. Antiques like this one can still function fairly well as heaters, provided they've managed to stay reasonably tight and free of cracks. However, unless you're determined to buy an original, you'd be better off with a copy. There are more than 100 exact reproductions[o] on the market, and some are even manufactured by the same companies that made the originals.

If a wood burner appeals to you, carefully read through page 128; it describes how to pick out the best spot in your house for a stove and how to choose the one that's right for

you, including information on materials, construction methods, accessories, and options.

Finally, taming fire so it works *for* you—not *against* you—requires specialized knowledge. Pages 130 and 131 discuss important subjects you should master if you plan to heat with wood: how to pick firewood, how to build the perfect fire, how to burn wood economically, and, perhaps most important, how to handle fire safely.

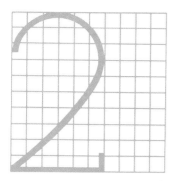

RECIPES FOR SUCCESSFUL EATING SPACES

Today's homes—and the way we live in them—have changed since the time when every house had a dining room proper. An entire room set aside just for meals is a luxury few of us can afford. But don't despair. When you look around your home, you'll find plenty of room for dining, even if there is no dining *room*. It may be in the entry way, part of the living room or even tucked out of sight between meals in a piece of double-duty furniture. This chapter presents a variety of gracious dining alternatives to the traditional formal dining room. Your own family's life-style and taste will determine the best place to dine and the most appropriate way to decorate the area.

ARRANGE FURNITURE CAREFULLY

A dining "room" that can seat four people in gracious style is hidden away in a handsome living room console, *below*. The console's center section stows five 14-inch extension pieces that fit together to make up a 79-inch-long surface for dining, or for a sumptuous buffet, *opposite*. When they are not drawn up for dining duty, the four matching chairs go their separate ways to become occasional seating pieces in the living room. The area rug and the large painting, which becomes a focal point for seated diners, create a true dining *area*, instead of merely a table opened in the living room.

If space permits, as it does in this room, keep the area in front of any convertible piece clear of other furnishings. You'll get maximum use and pleasure from a hideaway table if you don't have to take the time to move other furniture out of the way whenever you want to set the table up.

Room for expansion
Planning ahead is especially important when you're coaxing double-duty out of a single space. No matter where you find your dining room, it can be gracious and comfortable if you keep these requirements in mind:
• Allow at least 8 square feet to seat four people.
• Each chair needs approximately 3 feet of pullback room.
• Comfortable elbowroom at the table is about 24 inches per place setting. For example, a table that seats three down each side should be at least 72 inches long.
• Be sure to leave enough space between dining chairs (occupied) and the wall so you can pass through to easily serve your guests.
• Include the right kind of lighting for dining. That may be a ceiling-hung fixture, track lights, wall sconces, or, as shown on these pages, a table or floor lamp augmented by candlelight.

KEEP THINGS SIMPLE

Just as we've trimmed down our eating habits today, so can we streamline our eating *habitats*. If your taste and life-style don't favor a formal dining room, opt for simplicity. Choose furniture that requires a minimum of upkeep, then spread your table with easy-care linens topped with dishes that go from oven to table to dishwasher without worry. Simplicity is the keynote of good taste in the dining areas pictured on these pages.

Shop for surfaces that shrug off stains and resist scratches and burns. The slick laminate table in the elegantly simple dining room, *above*, wipes to a gleam at the touch of a damp cloth. If you prefer bare wood, *opposite*, protect the finish with wax or polyurethane varnish. Cane and chrome chairs, *above*, or wooden ones, *opposite*, eliminate upholstery upkeep. Carpets should be treated with soil-repellent finishes.

Simple necessities
Beyond the basic table-chairs arrangement, you'll need a convenient serving surface. This might be a traditional buffet, a pass-through service counter, or a flexible unit, such as the butler's tray, *opposite*, that stands near the dining table during meals, then folds or rolls away afterward.

Light it right
Good lighting—adequate, but not glaring—is essential for any eating space. Chandeliers or hanging fixtures are the most popular lighting for dining because they take up no table-top space. The green hanging fixture, *opposite*, was meant to shed light on an industrial scene, but here adds a sleek and simple touch to a dining area that's mellow enough with soft wood tones. Choose a fixture proportioned to the size of your table, bearing in mind that it's better to err on the large side than to lose an undersized fixture in an ocean of ceiling space.

How high you hang the light depends on both its size and shape. About 36 inches above the tabletop is a good rule of thumb. Just remember: You shouldn't have to look into the bulbs when seated or have to worry about hitting the fixture when you get up.

As a final convenience, install a dimmer switch. In an eating area that does double-duty, you can increase the light when you need it for work or soften it for dining.

PLAN FOR
EXPANDABILITY

Expandable tables provide spacious surfaces when you need them, yet take up little floor space the rest of the time. The drop-leaf table, a reliable standby of past generations, still works well for modern families. Tucked against a wall, in a hall, or behind a sofa, the table can be easily expanded by raising the leaves, and you're ready for dinner. Some dining tables have expansion leaves you can stow in a nearby closet; others store their leaves under the tabletop when you don't need them—a feature now available on some glass-topped models as well as on the more traditional wood tables. These pages offer other contemporary variations on the expandable theme.

The innovative space-stretcher, *below right*, starts with a clean-lined table designed by the famed Parsons School of Design in New York City. This elegant, right-angled table comes in every size, finish, and color. Here, it's even more versatile with an ingenious folding top. You'd never notice the table's hidden asset when it's pushed against the wall in the tiny room, *right*. But a few simple moves transform it into a full-fledged dining table that seats up to eight, *opposite*. The secret is two pieces of plywood, each the same size as the top (24x48 inches, in this case), hinged together and painted to match the table itself. Off-duty, the second top folds over on itself, with hinges out of sight against the wall. Set beneath a large mirror and flanked with wall sconces, the table becomes part of the furniture grouping opposite the seating area.

For dinner guests, the table moves out into the open, so there's room to flip open the top. Turning it 90 degrees on top of the table base makes a 48-inch-square dining surface. The Parsons table beneath provides a wobble-free base, and now the wall sconces provide intimate light for dining.

Parsons' combinations

A pair of matched Parsons tables can also solve the problem of where to put extra dinner guests. Because they work easily into almost any interior style, the tables can perform a number of tasks during the day: one as a desk, for example, the other as a sofa table or beside a bed. Pulled together, they are perfect for small dinner parties. Butted end-to-end, they become a long banquet table. And as supports for the opposite ends of a separate glass top, they can take on even more guests. For additional tricks with Parsons tables, see pages 34 and 35.

Dining in the round

You can turn a small, round occasional table into a spacious dining area, by having a larger top cut from ½-inch plywood (a 48-inch round will seat six comfortably). Pad the new top with felt stapled to the underside, and keep a large round cloth on hand. After dinner, the second top rolls into a convenient closet and the small table returns to its usual location.

Sit-down dining

For seating for impromptu dining, gather in all the occasional chairs you have dispersed throughout the house. Or position the dining table itself so that a convenient sofa or window seat can be pressed into service.

Where space is really at a premium, purchase chairs and stools that stack away in minimum space when they're not being used. Often designed by top architects and interior designers, stackables usually fit in well with either contemporary or traditional furnishings.

MERGE WITH OTHER AREAS

Don't get boxed in by the idea that a dining area needs to be enclosed by walls. Where space is limited—or where you want to eliminate barriers that make a room feel smaller than it really is—try merging a dining room with other areas in your home. The result may be an eat-in kitchen, family room, or living/dining combination. Neither partner in this venture needs lose its individual identity, and both can gain new spaciousness. The trick is to carefully define the dining area so you can enjoy an open arrangement without sacrificing mealtime intimacy. Two successful mergers are shown here, along with other suggestions for setting off your dining area without walling it in.

A successful dining area merger loosens boundaries, but not to the point where the new room feels too vast or undifferentiated for comfort.

Living and dining zones flow together, *below,* into one large, airy room that's gently—but definitely—separated for different activities by a railing around the raised dining area. The brass chandelier over the table and the area rug beneath it also serve to anchor the dining end of the room; wood flooring and off-white walls throughout link the two spaces.

In the room, *opposite,* the dining area is set apart by a lower ceiling and bare wood floor. Remodeling gave the living room a 17-foot vaulted ceiling; now the original 10-foot ceiling left in the dining area seems more intimate.

The two mergers shown both required structural changes—a raised dining platform in the first and altered ceiling heights in the second—but you can define your dining area without major construction. Here are three ways to go.

• *Paint and wall covering.* Vary the colors, patterns, or textures in the two areas. In the dining area, use a warmer shade, accent moldings, or put up wall covering. Maintain some continuity with the living area, however, or you'll lose the sense of spaciousness created by a merger.

• *Dividers.* Separate living and dining areas with a divider, but choose one that's low, or one that still lets you look from one space to the other. A rail does the job well, as would a low storage unit. An open-weave curtain, a partial divider of glass blocks, or a translucent screen are other options.

• *Floors.* Vary the surface of the floor. You can define the dining space with an area rug, *below,* or you may prefer an easy-care hard surface in the dining area, and the warmth of carpeting in the living area, *opposite.* Wood and carpeting aren't your only options; you can experiment with combinations of other materials, such as tile, stone, or brick.

CONSIDER
UNLIKELY
PLACES

When space is tight, it might make sense to relocate your dining area to a spot—perhaps away from the kitchen —where you have more room. Of course, dining in the outer reaches takes some careful planning to ensure that the host or hostess isn't constantly commuting to the kitchen. Different though they may be in mood— one's all business, the other's casually country—these two dining areas show how to take the necessities with you when you dine away from the kitchen.

The desk is always ready to serve double-duty as a dining table in the room *opposite*. High up under the eaves of a 75-year-old house, this remodeled room works all week as a home office/study, then converts into a hideaway for dinner parties on the weekend. An extra 2-foot-long section flips out from under the end of the table to add up to nearly 8 feet of dining space— enough for four persons seated, or for many more when the table is used as a buffet. When cleared of workaday debris, the 11-foot office system tucked under the angled wall becomes a backup serving

table. Office chairs take on leisure-time roles as super-comfortable dining chairs.

There is no chance the guests here will ever hear their host say, "Let's move into the other room where we can be more comfortable." With a wood-burning stove (not pictured here), soft overhead light (on a dimmer switch), plus a sound system, this already *is* the most comfortable area in the house.

If you're thinking of combining a dining area with a study or office, be sure to consider how frequently you'll be eating there. This study, *opposite*, works very well for weekend

entertaining, but would be less convenient for daily use. Eating three meals a day here would mean constantly clearing off and replacing any work that is in progress. If you choose to set up a similar room, provide another place for daily meals —perhaps a counter in the kitchen if your home is short on space.

New purpose for a porch
The porch on this page works well for both daily meals and entertaining. Since it's been double-glazed for year-round living, the family often heads here for meals—so often, in fact, that a big country cupboard has been moved in to simplify meal service. Along with its decorative collection of pottery and copper, the cupboard holds place settings and table linens. Here, the table is dressed for Sunday breakfast in a bright quilt, a cozy choice for a winter morning. Sensible touches that keep down upkeep in this surrogate dining room: the sisal rug, sturdy reproduction Windsor chairs, and an old wicker settee cushioned in durable red duck.

Breakfast in bed
Even a bedroom can do double-duty these days, especially for big-city dwellers who are perpetually short on space. Another incentive for dining in the bedroom is the proliferation of electronic entertainment gear—cable television, video tape recorders, videodiscs, and more—that is ending up in so many bedrooms today. If you like to take your dinner with TV, a double-duty desk/dining table in the bedroom is a convenient solution.

PLAY TRICKS
WITH TABLES

A big dinner party can suffer from too much togetherness. Instead of crowding everyone around one long table, consider assigning guests to conversation-size quartets or other smaller groupings. Folding card tables, draped with attractive cloths, offer one way to do this. Or multiply table space with matching tables like these.

For a short course in dining room arithmetic, study the equation on these pages. It shows two of the many ways you can solve different dining needs with the same four square tables. When pushed together in the center of this dining room, *right*, the champagne-colored tables merge into a single large square that could seat up to eight people with plenty of elbowroom—and without forcing anyone to straddle a table leg. Here, it's set for six, with one corner left free for an off-center centerpiece surrounded by glass candle holders.

Create mini-groupings

At formal dinner parties, where guests may be strangers to each other, they'll feel more at ease with some extra personal space. So instead of trying to crowd many guests around a single table, make them more comfortable—both physically and emotionally—by breaking the party up into smaller groups.

Dividing the tables to multiply the seating potential breaks the big square up into four separate dining sites with room for eight in just a little more floor space than the compact arrangement required. And, if overall space allows, you can separate the tables even further to make seating space for up to 16 guests without overcrowding.

The same idea works with smaller numbers of larger tables. For instance, two 4-foot squares are lightweight and easily pushed together for large dinner parties. Separate the tables so only two corners touch, and smaller groups can gather around one, leaving the other free for serving. A third option is to separate the tables completely so you can seat compatible groups at each.

INCLUDE OTHER ACTIVITIES

If space is at a premium in your house, why not put your eating area to work between meals? Plan a flexible arrangement, incorporate some double-duty pieces, and your eating area can fill a need that's not served elsewhere. The dining table/desk has been a classic site for homework for years, but those family members who are beyond school age can also benefit from similar strategies. A well-designed dining area can accommodate a variety of family activities and interests.

There's much more to the two eating areas shown here than meets the eye. The casual observer might see them as attractive areas in which to enjoy informal meals. But these rooms really go into action once the tables are cleared.

The builders of the kitchen addition, *opposite*, combine dining pleasure with business in their new 11x17-foot sky-lighted breakfast room. An office center runs wall-to-wall under the long window, with ample built-in storage space.

And there are more hidden assets to this addition: Dining stools tucked under the kitchen counter in the foreground put it to work for short-order service; a new entrance takes pressure off the front door; a coat closet offers lots of hanging space; and a generous pantry supplements kitchen storage.

Flexibility without adding on

Even if you can't add on, you can still create a successful multipurpose room like the one in the small home *below*. Six can dine at the table, which

serves as a desk between meals. The convertible sofa, convenient table, and television (unseen), provide a flexible sitting room that also works as a guest bedroom.

If you rarely use your present dining room for *dining*, because the table is usually covered with work, papers, and books that force you to eat elsewhere, then you have a good candidate for a multi-purpose eating space. Analyze the activities your family enjoys, then design your own other-than-dining room.

RELAX WITH
A COUNTRY
LOOK

We sense the touch of human hands in the worn farm tables and simple accessories—baskets, pewter, pottery, hand-loomed fabrics, hooked rugs—that are the essence of country style. Unself-conscious and undemanding, country dining encourages relaxed family meals. If you're not living in a farmhouse furnished with antiques, let a few authentic old pieces take center stage, and supplement them with replicas. Stock moldings, add-on beams, wood or brick flooring (or their resilient look-alikes) can transform a modern room into a dining area from yesteryear. If you enjoy crafts, design a multi-purpose country eating space, where your works-in-progress will become authentic accessories. And if you like what you see here, turn to pages 44 and 45 for more ideas about country decorating.

Country style really melds many styles from many countries—a cupboard from the French provinces, for instance, with natural quarry tiles from Mexico, and barnboard siding from a mid-America farm building.

The country look is in the *attitude* of the furnishings, not in their origin, or even their age. Today's versions of yesterday's furnishings make country style accessible even in a big-city high-rise. And acquiring authentic country furniture at auctions and barn sales can be an adventure in itself.

In the old farmhouse, *opposite*, both the furnishings and the setting are authentic. Lovingly restored—from hand-hewn beams still bearing adz marks down to wide-plank floors—this eat-in kitchen is the center of one family's home life. The old cookstove, open shelves filled with pottery, and rush-seated heirloom chairs under the simple wood table all contribute to the authentic country atmosphere.

Creating country

If your dining area is a plain contemporary space with no natural country attributes of its own, take a look at the dining room, *above*. For all its old-fashioned good looks, it's actually part of a relatively new home.

A combination of rustic gray woodwork and red mini-floral-stripe wallpaper, shutters at the windows, and a dark-stained wood floor provide an appropriate background for a few authentic old pieces: the solid pine harvest table and hoop-back Windsor chairs.

SET AN ELEGANT ATMOSPHERE

Because elegance transcends any one period or style of decorating, it's most accurately described in terms of timeless qualities: subtlety, refinement, taste, and formality. A sleekly contemporary dining room can be elegant. So can one that's richly traditional in mood and furnishings—and so can one that combines the best of both.

At first glance, this simply furnished dining room looks "traditional." Classic double-hung windows flank a fireplace; a formal "ancestor" portrait rests on the mantel; and a multi-tiered brass chandelier hangs above the table. But look closer and you'll see an elegant eclecticism that skillfully interweaves styles.

The centerpiece of the room is a modern, glass tabletop set on a pair of clear, semicircular plastic supports. Nontraditional accessories of rock and glass flank the portrait, providing subtle counterpoint to the contemporary table and looking especially dramatic against walls covered with Wedgwood blue fabric. Free-spiritedly placed on a diagonal in one corner, an antique cheval glass mirror further bridges the transition from traditional to contemporary.

Easy-care elegance
When it comes to keeping the sparkle in any eating space, it's nice to know that you needn't sacrifice convenience to achieve a formal look. The most elegant fabrics are now available with soil-repellent finishes, so velvets, brocades, and even suedes are practical choices for dining room chair upholstery.

Luxury-look linens for the table pop in and out of the washing machine with nary a wrinkle. Fine dishes with the elegant look of heirlooms go from oven to table to dishwasher. Modern technology has also given us brass that is prelacquered to prevent tarnish (check the manufacturer's instructions before serving food in it). Another boon to setting an elegant table without all the work: tarnish-preventive paper strips you merely toss in the drawer or buffet with sterling or plated silver.

ADOPT A CASUAL APPROACH

If you do little formal entertaining and prefer that elegant dinners be served at fancy restaurants, then you'll probably pass up a formal dining room at home and choose a comfortably casual eating area instead. Both dining areas shown here share family room territory—a practical and convenient combination.

Rich with natural materials and neutral colors, the family room *above* features lightweight rattan chairs that are easy to reposition around the room for after-dinner conversation. The wood floor, bare except for an exuberantly patterned rug, contributes to the easy informality of the room. Off-camera to the right, the kitchen is conveniently close at hand for quick service over a breakfast counter.

The all-white dining "room," *opposite*, is actually a very small space between the kitchen and family room. Yet it's been made to function in a big way for casual dining. The small table and folding chairs comfortably seat four without overcrowding the area. For larger gatherings, this spot converts to a bar or buffet.

Build in flexibility

A casual dining area should welcome drop-in guests and adapt easily to various activities, so choose tables that expand for dinner crowds and shrink for four-handed bridge. Have plenty of extra seating standing by. Include a counter, buffet, or serving cart to minimize trips to the kitchen.

Finally, don't install anything in a casual dining area that will demand undue care and attention. You'll be happier with surfaces such as tough synthetic tabletops, or real wood that has been coated with polyurethane to resist heat, wetness, and alcohol.

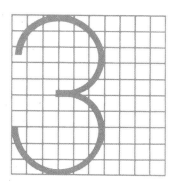

LIVE-IN ROOMS WITH THE LOOK YOU WANT

Every family needs a special room just to be a family in—a hands-on place where everyone can gather to enjoy games, hobbies, and good conversation. Like the room pictured here and those on the following pages, an effective live-in room will be the most inviting, most comfortable spot in the house. The emphasis is on livability, and, as you'll see in this chapter, livability comes wrapped in a variety of "looks."

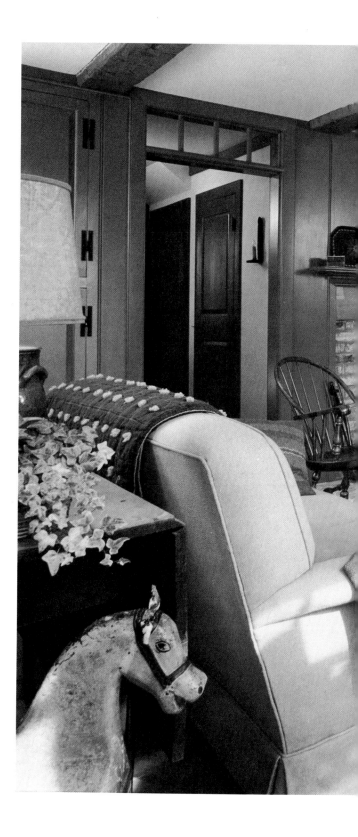

A country room has no
frills, so there's nothing
to put a crimp in your
comfort. It's a place that invites
you to unwind, relax, and be
yourself.

In every country room, the
past has a lot to do with the
present. Rooms like the one
shown here have their roots in
early American history, where
a single area served as kitch-
en, dining room, living room,
and sometimes even bedroom.
With all that living to do in one
place, furnishings had to be
practical.

For that reason, your twenti-
eth-century country room
should also be furnished to
take the kind of living you're
going to give it. Use sturdy
wood pieces with simple lines.
They'll fit both the look and the
livability of country decorating
if they have a few years on
them—or at least look like it.

• Choose surfaces of wood,
brick, stone, or white-washed
plaster. Walls and floors of a
country-style room should be
unpretentious and easy to take
care of.

• Keep fabrics looking rugged
and homespun, colors warm
and mellow. Accents are typically country if they're made of
wood, wrought iron, copper,
brass, tin, or stoneware.

• Be honest about the room's
design and function. Let family
activities become part of the
decor. For instance, crafts,
models, or collections make
good accessories in a country
room. So do the tools for any
form of handwork that you're
creating—from a basket of em-
broidery to a weaver's floor-
standing loom.

If there's one secret for
keeping a country room cozy,
it's this: don't get fancy with
furniture, fabrics, or room
arrangement. Keep everything
simple, rugged, and, above all,
comfortable.

TRY ECLECTICISM

Eclecticism is a tongue twister of a word, yet its meaning is simple. Eclecticism gives you the freedom to choose your favorite things from a number of periods and styles, rather than limiting yourself to only one. As you may have guessed, the key to this decorating look is you. But don't let this new-found freedom go to your head. Eclecticism does *not* mean putting whatever you like in a room, with no regard for the basics of good design. Too much diversity can result in a mish-mash of styles if one of two things isn't present: an innately fine sense of design or some guide-lines to help you combine the things you like into a cohesive room scheme. Generally, informal pieces from several styles mix well, just as formal ones do. Also, keep scale and proportion in mind as you group your furniture or accessories.

Although you can go in a number of directions when you're creating an eclectic style, these tips should help you find the mix that's best for you.

Think of function first

An eclectic room can be a frenetic combination of colors and designs—or it can be a relaxing, comfortable blend of elements. Base your choice on how you want the room to function, or more precisely, how you want to function in the room.

Because a live-in room is one in which you want to feel comfortable and relaxed, opt for a quiet environment—one with comfortable, easy-to-live-with colors and patterns in an open, uncrowded furniture arrangement. The room shown *at left* has both. The quiet beige-and-white print wall covering and white woodwork combine with the natural wood floor to provide a tranquil background for nubby, neutral-colored upholstered furniture and light wood pieces.

Make sure your family center has all the ingredients for living the good life. Plan plenty of comfortable seating, table space, work space, and storage space.

Be unorthodox

Eclectic decorating gives you a chance to use the interesting accessories that you've collected over the years.

How many families do you know who own an antique tricycle and a rifle-toting straw man, like those shown here? This family does and, more importantly, has no qualms about showing them off, along with a wicker laundry basket filled with yellow mums, and some other interesting basketry.

When designing your own room, keep two points in mind:
• A few large accessories add drama and give your room a finished look.
• Grouping smaller accessories together forms one large decorative "mass." Displaying them this way allows you to use some small pieces but also keeps the room free of clutter.

Play up contrasts

A room doesn't have to overwhelm you with color and pattern to be visually stimulating. An eclectic style often depends more on a contrast of textures than on flashy patterns.

In this room, for instance, the textured look of the mini-print wallpaper contrasts with the woodwork's sleek, white finish. Similarly, the shine of the natural wood floor plays off the texture and pattern of the kilim area rug. In addition, the nubby upholstery fabric looks even more textured when viewed against the smooth glass-topped table and the satin finish of the blond stools, rocker, and library table.

Match moods

An eclectic setting, despite its departure from formal decorating rules, shouldn't evoke a smorgasbord of moods. In an informal live-in room like the one here, keep the mood low-keyed and comfortable. Classic French armchairs wouldn't feel right in a room like this, but an old, handmade quilt from the attic would fit in splendidly.

Coordinate colors

One way to unify a room filled with disparate items is to repeat a basic color scheme. Develop a simple plan, using only a few colors and repeating each one to give the room a well-balanced look.

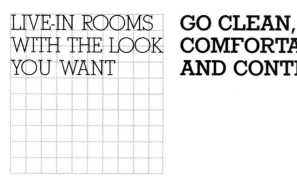
GO CLEAN,
COMFORTABLE,
AND CONTEMPORARY

The clean lines and simple styling of contemporary furniture naturally lend themselves for use in a live-in room. The number of furniture pieces is generally kept to a minimum; each is beautifully designed and unwaveringly functional. At the same time, there's a certain air of importance about each piece, especially when it's given enough space to be noticed.

A contemporary room should not be uncomfortably cold or sterile. If a room is meant to be a spot for reading and relaxing, adequate and comfortable seating is essential. The room *above* features a love seat, rocker, and fireside chair, while the room *opposite* features two comfortable one-armed sofa/chaises.

If your family enjoys reading, space for storing books is also needed. In a contemporary setting, however, bookshelves are no-nonsense units—compact and utilitarian, like the ones in the room *above*.

Be sure the room has the right kind of lighting. Don't worry about pretty little decorative lights. Use what works best, placing lights where you need them. In the room on the opposite page, two industrial-type light fixtures drop beside each sofa, and both rooms pictured have ceiling track lights to provide special lighting accents.

If your family center is a place to watch television, play games, or work on hobbies and crafts, then everything should be near at hand in easily accessible storage. Or, let simple, functional objects, like stereo equipment or craft tools, stand on their own as useful and attractive accessories. Clear-cut, honest design like this makes contemporary so easy to live with.

Don't worry about the numbers game

How much furniture you pack into a room isn't important. Instead, contemporary design means paring everything down to the bare essentials, so a room has everything it needs, but no more—nothing to distract you or to cause additional upkeep.

If your live-in room is small, contemporary is a good choice. The fewer the objects, the larger a room appears to

be. Here are some other tips to make a small room look bigger:
• Pull furniture away from the walls to create an illusion of added space.
• Use white or light colors to make a room—and its furnishings—appear larger.
• Leave windows bare to give a room an open, airy quality.

Concentrate on shapes

When a room is free of everything that's superfluous, what's left takes on new visual importance. For that reason, each design element in a contemporary room—material, color, texture, and, most often, shape—has its own special beauty.

Let your eyes roam over the shapes in the living room, *opposite*. Notice the stacked circular tables, the multi-level magazine holder, and the unique shape of the seating pieces. The same thing is true in the room *at left*. The lines and curves of the bentwood rocker, the fireside chair, and even the pendulum clock mounted over the fireplace all add interest to the room.

Placement matters

In contemporary design, where you put the objects in a room is just as important as what those objects are. A rule of thumb: give everything enough space to develop its own visual impact. Look at the room shown *opposite*, for example. In a more traditional setting, the stack of tables, with its stylized arrangement of red tulips, would probably be tucked into a corner or used at the end of a sofa. But when placed in the middle of the room, it becomes more dramatic and more important.

FURNISH WITH
TRADITIONAL
CLASSICS

Traditional design is a traditional favorite. Generations of American families have found it to be a comfortable, practical, and eminently sensible way to turn their houses into homes. And because it's as popular as ever, this classic style is a down-to-earth choice for an up-to-date live-in room.

Too often, people think that traditional classics are museum pieces or, at the very least, furnishings that belong in only the most elegant home and not in rooms geared to family living. If that's what you believe, the room pictured here may change your mind. Antiques and American primitives cozy up to each other, creating a wonderfully inviting room. There's nothing standoffish about it. Instead, it exudes a warmth that's hard to match in any other style.

Surface savvy

The style, color, and design of your room's surfaces help set the tone for your live-in room's comfort and practicality. Look at this room as an example.

If the walls had been finished in rich damask wall covering, with yards of velvet or antique silk at the window, the room would become so formal that living in it would be difficult. On the other hand, the surfaces used here—plain white walls with simple accents of colonial green wood trim —make the room cheerily unpretentious, a perfect background for the comfortable furnishings.

In the same way, the wrong surface treatment could easily transform the camel-back sofa and antique Queen Anne chairs into stiff period pieces. If a room is going to be lived in, then its upholstered furniture must have practical cover fabrics, and not the moires or damasks so often seen on traditional furniture in formal settings. Practicality dominates the room in this photograph.

A stylized beige-and-white floral fabric covers the antique sofa, while an upbeat beige-and-white oversize check covers the seats of the antique chairs. To minimize upkeep, both fabrics are protected by a stain repellent.

Warm up to warm colors

Color plays a major role in making a room seem warm and inviting. If you want a room to be relaxing and comfortable, be sure to choose warm, natural colors—earth tones, browns, ochres, rusts, oranges, and reds.

The room shown here has a traditional color scheme using beige, clay, and terra cotta, with a hint of muted green added. All the colors are pulled together in the hand-braided rug and are echoed throughout the fabric, accessories, painted trim, and wood furniture. As a result, nothing in the room is out of step with the warm, subdued color scheme.

Break with tradition

Traditional furniture usually is arranged in a symmetrical, formal way. By throwing out the old rules and arranging furniture and accessories in a more relaxed, informal manner, you create a room that's inviting to live in.

Try another way to put classic furniture pieces at ease in your live-in room: blend them with more contemporary pieces. Add things like American primitives, Indian baskets, forged metals, or hand-dipped candles. You'll find that high-style traditional and more modest pieces not only blend well but the combination is more comfortable than either style would be on its own.

COORDINATE
WITH FABRICS

Fabric is one of the most useful tools a home decorator can have. It's the only design element that can give your room color, pattern, and texture —plus softness. And it's the only decorating treatment you can use on walls, windows, and furniture. In other words, fabric is versatile. It can play leading roles (setting a room's color scheme, for example), or it can play supporting parts (sofa pillows acting as color accents). Try the ideas on this page, and you're sure to be satisfied with fabric's performance.

Putting a room together is like darning a stocking. There has to be a common thread that weaves in and out of an area, pulling in loose ends and tying them together into one neat design package. In many rooms, fabric can be that thread.

Where to fabricate

There are several logical places for fabric to appear in a room—on furniture, at windows, as table skirts, or as accent pillows. In addition to these expected places, there are some less familiar spots for fabric. For instance, fabric makes a great wall covering, either glued or stapled to the wall, or shirred on curtain rods attached near the ceiling and the floor. Or, for a real eye-catcher, use fabric on the ceiling of your room.

For interesting accents, try covering a lampshade with fabric. Or use fabric to mat a print or photo, or to serve as place mats and napkins if you also dine in your live-in room.

Each time you use fabric in a room, you have another opportunity to coordinate the area—providing, of course, you're using the right fabric in the right location.

Here's some information to help you when you're selecting and using fabrics.

Picking and choosing

Selecting a color is your first decision. If your family is going to spend a lot of time in a room, select fabrics that are practical in color, that won't show soil easily, and that fit your personality and style of living.

Warm colors—yellow, orange, and red—make a room brighter and livelier, while cool colors—blue, green, and violet—make a room appear serene and relaxing.

Regardless of color, if the fabric you choose is a solid (without a pattern), consider selecting one with some surface texture. Textured fabrics are usually heavier and, especially on seating pieces, will wear better than a fine-weave fabric.

Choosing a pattern is also an important decision. For an informal room, choose casual patterns, such as checks and plaids. Or use small prints, such as tiny florals or geometric designs.

The *style* of your fabric window designs or furniture covers should be in keeping with the character and function of the room.

For instance, the informal room pictured on these two pages uses a window design that is traditionally thought of as a formal style—or it would be if it had been executed in the expected way. However, instead of a swag and a pair of side jabots hung over elegant draperies, the family chose a swag and only one jabot hung above inside-mounted shutters. The effect is casual and imaginative. (A little secret to the success of this symmetrical window design is the red band of color on the crown molding. It moves the eye from one window to the other and ties them together.)

The right combination

Combining several prints within a room will be an easy task if you choose one of these ways to go.
• Keep the blend of colors the same in all prints. In this room, the blue with red fabric is a perfect counterpoint to the red with the blue print.
• Keep the size and type of patterns the same, and combine different colors.
• Keep both the colors and the pattern size similar.

USE MODULAR FURNITURE FOR FLEXIBILITY

If your furniture is stuck firmly in the middle of the road—or room—with a definite case of the decorating blahs, try using a changeable, rearrangeable modular system. Shaped and sized to come together in almost any way you choose, modular configurations allow you to buy only the pieces you need. They fit almost any budget, any space, and any style. In fact, you can furnish entire rooms with modular upholstered pieces, or storage units that can be combined in different ways to create a variety of looks and versatile room arrangements.

No matter how much a modular room changes, it will always stay the same—flexible.

Basic building blocks

Each modular unit is designed to take the same amount of floor space as the other units, no matter what their shape. This means you can add to your arrangement in either direction or replace one piece with another to change the look of a grouping.

Seating pieces are available in a few basic shapes: a square with no back or arms, a square with a back, and a square with both a back and an arm. The latter piece can serve as a corner unit in an L-shaped grouping, or two can flank a line of pieces, creating arms for a sofa. Two of them used side by side create a love seat with back and arms.

The room *at right* (and on the cover) is a model of modular design. Placed on an area rug in this living room, six pieces of furniture form up-to-date comfort. The basic units making it all take shape are those mentioned above: a square, a square with a back, and a square with a back and an arm (corner piece). The upholstered tables provide extra flexibility. (They're included in some manufacturers' lines.) In the room shown here, one unit serves as a coffee table; the other is a side table between two groups of seating modules. These six pieces are nearly all the furniture this room needs.

More than seating

Modular seating pieces are great for furniture arranging flexibility, but don't stop there. The same versatility is available in modular storage units. In addition to those featuring bookshelves and cabinets, there are others that include such extras as bars, desks, stereo-TV cabinets, and glass shelves with display lighting.

Line a whole wall with modular storage pieces, and they look as though they're built in. But you're actually free to move them—easily—whenever you wish.

What an arrangement

If your furniture arrangement is bogged down by a beefy sofa and a couple of hulking chairs, you're going to think twice before moving anything. Modular furniture, however, is often constructed of plastic foam, making it featherlight to move. Even without this type of construction, it's a lot easier to move just one module at a time than to push around pieces the size of standard sofas and love seats.

With this kind of mobility, arranging modular furniture is no problem. If a room is small, simply tighten up the grouping and snug it up to the walls. If your live-in room has more space to spare, loosen up the modular grouping and float it in the center of the room. Another advantage to this furniture is that it's finished on all four sides, making freestanding groupings of storage pieces, for instance, attractive from any angle.

All the standard shapes for furniture arrangements are possible with modulars. They're naturals for L-shaped or U-shaped furniture arrangements. Or place two separate groups of units opposite each other for a parallel arrangement. For a more unusual scheme, group modular units to form a square, with just a walk-through space into an area for casual conversations. (For more about modular furniture, see pages 72 and 73.)

ORGANIZE FOR
ACTIVITIES

Living in a room involves considerably more than sitting down to read the paper or, on occasion, entertaining a few friends. *Really* living in an area means equipping it to handle your whole family's daily activities. And the key to doing that right—and making the room look good—is organization.

If there's dust on your "someday-I've-got-to-get-organized" plaque, toss it out and get started. Organization can get you living in every inch of a room's space. Start by considering the activities your family pursues.

Make a list

The first step toward organizing your family living center is to list the things you do there. Then note the equipment and supplies each activity requires.

Next, analyze just how important any one activity is to the overall scheme of the room. If the whole family enjoys doing the same thing and it's important to your style of living, you may want to build your live-in room around it. On the other hand, if you've listed several activities—or if those activities are just pleasant extras—you'll want to find ways to tuck them into what's basically an all-purpose room.

Create a floor plan

Once more, study the lists you've made. Will you need furniture or large pieces of equipment? For instance, the room *at right* was planned to accommodate a floor-standing loom. If music is your family's hobby, you'll probably want to find room for a piano or organ.

But, while you'll want the equipment or instruments to be part of the room scheme, you probably won't treasure a loom or harp in areas you'll talk in or walk through.

Depending on how important the activity is to the purpose of the room, you'll have to arrange the furniture so that it's either built around the piano, or is included in a more subtle way. (To learn more about activity-centered rooms, see Chapter 7—"Rooms For Fun & Games.")

Decide on storage

While you can store tatting or petit point in small boxes or baskets, for the most part, family activities will need extra storage space. In many cases, it has to be specialized.

First, determine what has to be stored, then decide whether to create open or closed storage. Is what you're storing attractive enough to be placed on open shelves, or is it better hidden behind closed doors? For example, in the home office *opposite*, all you have to do is close the drop-front cabinets to hide clutter within. Whatever type of storage you choose, it should be easily accessible from the activity area.

Take another look at what you're going to store. Will you need to plan customized shelves or cabinets for oversized items, such as a projection screen, large books, or music stands? Will you require specialized drawers for papers, patterns, or tools? What about compartments for storing yarn or fabric? What you store influences the kind of storage space you plan and where you place it.

Don't destroy the evidence

Don't tell the youngsters to pick up their toys—at least not all the time. Live-in room activities, projects "in the works," or the not-yet-finished chess game can serve as attractive, mood-making accessories. Too much neatness is sterile and less cheery. Evidence of an active family is more appealing visually with today's casual decorating styles. For instance, in the room *below,* an arrangement of baskets heaped with balls of weaving yarn makes an interesting accessory.

On the other hand, if neatness is one of your virtues, you may prefer an area with ample closed storage like the one *opposite*. Because it's meant to be an office, in part, that orderly look is just what the homeowner wanted.

BRING THE OUTDOORS IN

There's a little naturalist in everyone. Even the most hardened urban dweller occasionally longs for the cool, relaxing beauty of the outdoors. One solution, of course, is to bring the outdoors in and create a natural look in the comfort of an insect- and climate-controlled room. Although the final effect may be simulated, for most of us, it's the best of both worlds.

When camping out is a bit more uncivilized than you care to be, consider ways to bring the outdoors inside.

Do it architecturally

If you're designing your own home or adding on a family center, the easiest way to live with nature is to plan a room with plenty of windows, preferably floor to ceiling. The room *at right* starts out with that architectural advantage, but there are plenty of other ideas that can make a room feel and look "outdoorsy" without knocking out walls and adding new glass.

Just in case you *are* blessed with a wide expanse of window, don't fence it in with heavy window treatments. Keep window designs architectural and to a minimum.

Do it horticulturally

Even with more walls than windows in your family center, you can still bring the outdoors in. Just make several trips to a local greenhouse and literally "plant" your live-in room.

Plan a variety of greenery. Group floor-standing plants of several heights; drop plants from the ceiling; and add potted plants on shelves, pedestals, or other staging devices. (More about plants can be found on pages 60-63.)

Make sure there's enough natural light for the plants. If not, use artificial grow lights, placed to provide a substitute for the sun.

Do it visually

There are tricks to creating an outdoor atmosphere that go beyond either interior or exterior plantings.

Work on the room's surfaces. In the one pictured here, the walls and ceiling have been completely covered with white lattice. The effect is that of an interior gazebo, and you can create it in any room, regardless of its exposure to the outside world.

To make a room look like a patio, consider using brick or stone on the floor. In addition, exterior siding or shingles on the wall help to create the feeling of a porch setting.

The furniture you choose also can enhance the outdoor effect. Try typically "outdoor" furniture materials, such as wicker, rattan, plastic-coated wire, wrought iron, or redwood. Use glass-topped tables, baskets, and clay pottery for accessories, and choose upholstery calculated to coordinate with the outdoor theme. In this room, deep forest-green corduroy covers the sofa and rattan chair cushions. The fabric is casual enough to fit into the natural scheme of things, and the color is as fresh as that of any plant growing either in or outside the room.

Keep the room's colors lush and cool or sunstroked and warm—depending on whether your idea of the great outdoors is a shadowy glen or an open meadow.

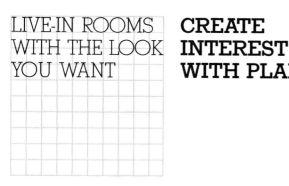
CREATE
INTEREST
WITH PLANTS

Collecting plants can be a rewarding hobby. They can add a touch of life—or a spot of color—to a room. But to the wise home decorator, that lush greenery also gets put into service in dozens of other ways. When you know something about plants and how to use them for the look you want, you'll find that investing in a few growing things is a good first step toward creating a livelier live-in room that your whole family will enjoy.

Living, growing plants are a joy just to have around. Beyond that, they can make big contributions to nearly any decorating scheme. Read the advice below and you may develop a budding interest in using plants to make a room live right.

Furnish with plants
In a room with little furniture, plants are perfectly acceptable stand-ins. Large, floor-standing varieties, those referred to as "architectural plants," are natural replacements for furniture. But they're not your only option. You can fill empty spaces effectively by grouping plants and elevating them on risers of different heights. Or simply collect plants and arrange them on a tabletop, as in the room *opposite*.

In addition to furnishing a room, plants serve other decorating functions. For example, leafy foliage helps soften the hard lines of furniture shapes and walls. Place plants between two areas of a room and they'll act as a natural divider. Or position them as barriers to direct the flow of traffic. And, when used in front of a window, plants become a light-filtering window design.

Plant patterns in a room
Add a plant, and you add both pattern and texture to a room. Because plants have characteristic shapes, each creates a unique impression—soft and fuzzy, frail and wispy, rugged and prickly. Choose plants with different textures, and arrange them so groupings are visually interesting.

Plants can provide color accents in a room, as well. Not all plants are the same shade of green, nor are they even all green. Use varying shades of light and dark green, then add some colored foliage. You'll

find the plant groupings more interesting—both as botanical displays and as room accents.

Talked about plants
Few people own original da Vinci paintings or Renaissance tapestries. Yet everyone is able to afford a plant, and no two plants are alike—each is an original. Some plants are exotic, even rare. If you own an unusual bit of botany, showcase it the same way you would a fine painting. Place it in an attention-getting location, and light it to its best advantage.

To spotlight a featured plant, use a grow light, rather than an ordinary light bulb. It creates the same visual effect but gives your plant light that's more like the sun's.

Arranging plants
Plants, like furniture or accessories, need to be arranged properly in a room.
• Don't scatter small potted plants throughout an area.

An isolated plant will look lost in a room. Instead, group several plants into one cohesive design element.
• Group plants of various heights and colors to avoid monotony. To vary their heights in the room, elevate plants on pedestals, cubes, boxes, bricks, or overturned clay pots.

Be interested in your plants
No plant will decorate a room well if you skimp on its care.
• Don't forget: plants in small pots dry out faster than those in large ones. Water them more frequently.
• Hanging plants dry out faster than those in cooler, floor-level locations. Water appropriately.
• If your room doesn't provide adequate natural light, use grow lights.

On the next two pages you'll find detailed information on how to keep architectural plants healthy and happy.

(continued)

CREATE
INTEREST
WITH PLANTS

(continued)

Many people who depend on plants to make a room livable are greenhorns when it comes to taking care of them. They don't have green thumbs; they're all thumbs. They water their plants too often or not enough. They don't give them adequate light, or they scorch them with far too much.

Not all plants require the same conditions to grow properly. What is healthy for one variety may be harmful for another. If you care enough about plants to make them integral parts of your decorating scheme, you'll need special knowledge to raise them right.

FAVORITE ARCHITECTURAL PLANTS

	CHARACTERISTICS	LIGHT/OTHER NEEDS
SHORT AND BUSHY (up to 3 feet)		
Chinese evergreen	Tapered leaves dip at tip.	Tolerates low light and humidity. Keep evenly moist.
Jade tree	Thick, fleshy leaves.	Prefers full sun. Water when soil dries.
Parlor palm	Grows very slowly. Reaches only 3 to 4 feet.	Requires bright to medium light. Keep evenly moist.
Yucca	Sharp, rigid leaves, 10 to 18 inches long.	Prefers bright light and porous soil. Water when soil dries.
MEDIUM HEIGHT (up to 6 feet)		
Aralia	Lacy leaves.	Bright, indirect light. Keep evenly moist.
Dracaena	Long leaves, some speckled, some edged in white or red.	Medium or bright light. Keep evenly moist.
Norfolk Island pine	Evergreen, with boughs growing in tiers.	Likes bright, indirect light. Water when soil dries.
Philodendron	Leathery, usually glossy leaves.	Medium filtered or bright, indirect light. Keep moist.
Schefflera	Glossy leaves on brittle stems.	Bright light, either direct or indirect. Water when dry.
INDOOR TREES (to the ceiling)		
Ficus (figs)	Graceful shape. Plain or variegated varieties.	Needs bright, indirect light. Keep evenly moist.
Ficus (rubber tree)	Large, leathery leaves growing from a single stem.	Needs bright, indirect light. Keep evenly moist.
Palm	Tree varieties grow quickly, put out new growth in winter.	Needs bright, indirect light. Keep evenly moist.

SELECTED SPECIES	SPECIAL CARE	GROWTH CONTROL
Variegated, Silver King.	Can be grown in water. Watch for mealybugs, scale, and virus infection.	Prune when plant becomes leggy.
	Watch for scale, mealybugs, and edema.	Prune if needed; however, charm of this plant comes from its natural shape.
	Subject to red spider mites and scale.	Palms cannot be pruned.
Adam's needle, spineless.	Avoid direct drafts. Subject to thrips.	Cut back when too tall. New top growth will start where cut.
Balfour, ming, false.	Red spider mites, scale, and thrips are common pests.	Cut back if plant grows too tall.
Corn plant, dragon tree, gold-dust, red-margined.	Clean leaves to promote breathing. Watch for red spider mites.	Cut back if plant grows too tall.
	Water less often in winter.	Cannot be pruned. Keep in small pot to retard growth if needed.
Fiddleleaf, heartleaf, saddleleaf, and Red Emerald.	Train to climb pole.	Prune as needed to control growth.
	Keep an eye out for scale, spider mites, and aphids.	Prune as needed.
Creeping, climbing, fiddleleaf, weeping, and mistletoe.	Pests include scale and thrips. Weeping figs lose leaves if light is too dim.	Prune as needed.
	Avoid drafts. Subject to thrips.	Cut back. Stalk will ooze milky fluid when cut. Rub wound with ice to seal.
Areca, bamboo, Chinese fan, fishtail, and sentry.	Plant in porous soil. Don't let pots stand in water.	Don't prune. Slow growth by keeping in smaller pot.

Large, architectural plants may become bigger than you bargained for. The chart on these two pages provides helpful information on common architectural plants, including a section on plant growth.

Get acquainted

Treat your plants as individuals. Although it's not necessary to master a long list of scientific Latin names, any conscientious plant owner should at least be familiar with each plant's common name.

Find out, too, the origin of each variety. It will have a bearing on how you care for the plant. For example, plants that originated on the shady floor of a jungle will need less light than those that once grew in sunny meadows or on an arid desert.

Protect your plants

To a degree, each plant is susceptible to insects and disease. Find out which bugs and illnesses may bother the plants you own. Learn the symptoms of infestation and the ways to cure it. Keeping your plants in good health will generally help them resist many problems, but even that is no guarantee. So watch them carefully, and act quickly to treat harmful conditions.

Special care

Some plants, especially architectural plants, need trimming or pinching back. Once you know how high and wide you want them to be, learn how to control their growth.

And, if you're interested in propagating new plants, find out how each variety can be reproduced—by cuttings, division, or air-layering. (For information about greenhouses, see pages 116 and 117.)

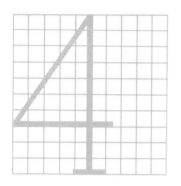

CHOOSING & BUYING FURNITURE

Important purchases demand important information to back them up. Most people don't buy a new house after a quick walk around the exterior or put down thousands of dollars on a car just because it "seems to look O.K." The same goes for any furniture purchase. To be a savvy buyer, you need more than vague ideas about what you want, where you want to put it, and how much you can afford. This chapter tells how to go beyond appearances to be sure that what you're buying is really worth the money you're spending.

UPHOLSTERED PIECES

Before you set out for your local furniture store, sit down and review your family's needs and tastes, your space limitations, and your lifestyle. If you have any young children and enjoy a casual environment, you'll need durable furniture that offers sink-in comfort and easy care. High-style upholstery pieces covered with luxury fabrics, on the other hand, better suit more formal situations.

Measure your rooms carefully. There's nothing worse than bringing home new furnishings that don't suit the size or scale of your home—unless it's pieces that won't even fit through the door!

Underneath it all

When you're ready to begin the search for the furniture that's right for you, remember this maxim about upholstered pieces: What you see isn't necessarily what you get. Under all the pretty fabric is a reflection of materials and workmanship that can mean the difference between a beautiful buy and a bad bargain. So find out the inside story first.

Except for polyurethane foam and molded plastic furniture, most upholstered pieces have the same general construction: a frame, springs, padding, and a cover fabric. Different manufacturers, employing different levels of workmanship, use different kinds of material. The products, of course, vary widely in quality—and in price. The key to telling the difference is knowing how good furniture is put together.

The frame—be sure to know the angles

Traditionally, high-quality furniture frames have been made of seasoned kiln-dried hardwood, which doesn't warp under normal conditions. Metal and polystyrene are also used in some cases.

You won't, in fact, be able to *see* the frame of the piece you're looking at, but check the manufacturer's catalog; it may have drawings of how the frame is constructed.

Most quality frames are an interlocking set of pieces cut to fit together like a puzzle, not just butted up against each other. The pieces of a good frame are also linked by spiral-groove dowels or by double dowels.

Corner blocks offer another important clue about how a chair or sofa comes together—and stays together. In the best furniture, they're screwed and glued in place, usually backed up by a piece of plywood for a nice, precise fit. Corner blocks that are only stapled won't be as stable in the long run.

Legs must be sturdy, too. They should be either extensions of a solid frame or made of interlocking pieces that are jointed to the frame with heavy-duty construction. Legs that are simply screwed into the frame or into metal plates attached to the frame may weaken and wobble in time.

Springs you need to know

Most upholstered pieces have a series of springs supporting the cushioning. The most common are coil springs and sinuous, or non-sag, springs. Many manufacturers use more than one kind within the same chair or sofa. A certain type may give the piece a special shape, while another adds resiliency.

In well-made furniture with coil springs, many coils cover the platform. Inferior pieces have coils that are placed farther apart.

How coil springs are bound together is another sign of quality. The best method is an eight-way tie, using substantial cord, with each cord lashed firmly to the frame. Springs tied only four ways aren't as stable.

Most good furniture also features steel bands reinforcing the underside of the springs, and polypropylene, burlap, or some other fabric covering the top side. Webbing under the springs is another checkpoint. Whatever material is used (jute is traditional; polypropylene, newer), it should be laced or woven tightly together; the bands shouldn't be so far apart you can stick your hand between them.

Sinuous springs, which look like wavy lines of heavy metal wire, offer substantial support but aren't as resilient as coils. Often, they're found in the *back* of upholstered pieces.

Some upholstered furniture has fabric slings that support the cushions. This type of construction is low in cost, but the final product is less comfortable and durable than one with a conventional spring system.

Cushioning or padding

Quality furniture has two or three layers of padding, often with a layer of fabric between them. Less careful manufacturers often will skimp on the cushioning, but thickness (and comfort) are things that you can judge for yourself.

Cushiony comfort can be traditional or more contemporary, as with the chair illustrated *at right*.

(continued)

UPHOLSTERED PIECES
(continued)

- *Spring-down* cushioning is found only in expensive furniture. Individual coil springs are put into muslin covers. In some cases, the coils may have polyurethane-filled centers. Then these muslin-covered coil springs on a block of polyurethane are inserted into a casing of fabric. Down is then blown into a channeled, down-proof muslin casing and the spring-filled core is wrapped with it.
- *Polyurethane* is the most popular material for cushions. Often called "polyfoam," it is strong, lightweight, and flexible. Polyurethane offers a soft, yet resilient, cushion, won't cause allergies, and stands up well to most upholstery cleaning solutions.
- *Latex foam rubber* cushions are more expensive than polyurethane but may be more versatile. They are available in a variety of shapes and are very comfortable, although the foam tends to crust and crystallize after a·few years.
- *Flame-retardant* cushions have become popular in recent years—and, in some cases, mandatory. Flame-retardant cushions either are chemically treated to retard burning when exposed to an open flame, or inherently do so. (Cushions covered with wool upholstery are an example of the latter.) There is no perceptible difference in the appearance of a cushion that has been treated.

Your cushions should be wrapped with a protective covering—preferably a non-woven fabric—so the filling won't bunch up and the outer fabric won't buckle.

Seat cushions will probably be firmer than back cushions, but both should offer firm, resilient support. The filling should be evenly distributed.

Facts about fabrics

Unlike other parts of upholstered furniture, you can *see* the fabric easily. Even so, different fabrics have different strengths and weaknesses.

First check the hangtag for the fabric's fiber content. If the furniture is made of natural fibers like wool, cotton, or silk, the upholstery will be supple to the touch and offer good wear under light-to-moderate use. Cover fabrics woven of synthetic fibers like nylon, rayon, olefin, polyester, or acetate will provide good wear even with heavy use and will also resist fading better than natural fiber fabrics.

Blends—fabrics made of two or more fibers—combine the good characteristics of the fibers they contain. Upholstery woven of cotton and polyester, for instance, offers the crisp comfort and good color rendition of cotton and the strength and durability of polyester.

Fabrics also should hold their shape, even after being pulled in all directions. Test a fabric by holding it up to the light. Tightly woven fabrics don't let much light shine through and will wear better than loosely woven types.

Many fabrics have chemical finishes that resist stains. However, some fibers—olefin, for example—naturally repel stains and don't need additional help. Some finishes fend off both oil and water stains; others resist only one (usually water).

What if you don't find the fabric you want? Some retailers have an inventory of upholstered furniture, but to get just what you want, you may have to order it specially, which may incur greater expense and longer delivery times.

Piecing it all together

Now that you understand something about the reality behind the appearance of upholstered furniture, how do you test a lovely sofa or chair when you're shopping?

First, sit down on it. Wiggle, squirm, and bounce on it. Take off your shoes and curl up on it. These are the most important tests you can make. If the furniture's not comfortable to you—or to other members of your family—it's not worth the money.

While you're wiggling and bouncing, listen. The frame shouldn't creak, and the springs shouldn't squeak.

Now lean and push against the back of the furniture. It shouldn't give. If the piece has proper padding, you won't be able to feel the springs and frame. Nor should you detect metal or wood through the padding and upholstery.

Pay attention to patterns. Carefully matched, they're a sign of good workmanship. Plaids, stripes, and checks should flow together from the top of the back to the floor. In well-made furniture, flower patterns are centered on cushions and along the back panel above them. Patterns on arms match, and the deck (the area under the seat cushions) is covered in a matching color. Patterns on the back of the furniture piece should match closely, so you can move the furniture anywhere in the room.

Not only do patterns match in carefully crafted furniture, but any details—exposed wood, color accents, or carvings—should be uniform over the entire piece.

Skirts should be straight, and, to be durable, they must be lined. If the piece is tufted, wrinkles should spread away from the tuftings. The buttons should be securely attached.

Cushion covers with zippers fit better and are smoother than those without any. They also permit you to straighten the filling, if necessary. Zippers do not necessarily mean the covers are washable, however. Read the fabric care instructions to be sure.

Inspect the welting (the cord covering the seams). It should be straight and neatly sewn. The smaller the welt, the smaller the seam, and generally the better the furniture.

Finally, check all exposed seams. If there seem to be more than are necessary to sew the material together, the manufacturer may be skimping. Gently pull at the seams; the stitches should be tight.

What price is right?

Fortunately, there are so many different styles in so many different price ranges that you should be able to find well-crafted furniture of all kinds—not only upholstered goods—even if you have relatively little money to spend. Simply determine what you can pay, then compare the quality of the merchandise available in that range, selecting the best you can afford.

The biggest cost by far in producing furniture is labor. The more complicated the design, the more work goes into it, and the higher the price tag. So choosing simple designs can save you money.

Buying at sales is another good way to keep prices where you want them. From manufacturer to you, most furniture pieces are marked up 100 percent or more. If you can put off a purchase until a sale is on, there's a good chance you'll save 10 to 20 percent off the list price—even as much as 40 to 60 percent at clearance and inventory time. Generally, you'll find the biggest bargains during winter and early spring (January through March) and in August.

CASE GOODS

Case goods (unupholstered pieces of furniture) include cabinets, chests, desks, étagères, sideboards, wall units, and tables. Shopping for them can be less complicated than choosing their cushiony cousins. After all, the framework of a chair or a sofa is buried under fabric and stuffing, while you can actually *see* a cabinet or chest in its true form. Even so, first impressions can be deceiving. As you shop for case goods, there are things to look for—and look out for. Here are some tips.

Careful shopping for case goods is like careful shopping for upholstered furniture. You must be prepared.

Measure the room or rooms where you plan to put the new furniture. Also note any idiosyncratic architectural features. A slanted ceiling or large fireplace, for example, may affect your original ideas.

Check traffic flow in the house; new pieces shouldn't be stumbling blocks. Measure doorways. Will your beautiful bookcase even make it in? Will the doors of the piece open in the right direction for your planned arrangement?

Study a few model rooms and page through your favorite magazines to see which styles you like. Then pick out stores with good reputations, and check for brand names. Even though most case goods don't have written guarantees, the best stores and manufacturers will stand behind their furniture.

Ask questions, inspect furniture in a number of stores, and then ask more questions. The salespeople in reputable stores should know their products well. And be sure to read all labels and hangtags. Page 69 explains what they can tell you about wood furniture.

(continued)

CASE GOODS

(continued)

Of course, wood, though still the people's choice, isn't the only material being used to make furniture. Manufacturers are also employing rattan, wicker, leather, plastic, metal, and glass, either alone or in combination with wood. (For more about wicker and rattan, see pages 70 and 71.)

Checkpoints

Inspect all furniture inside and out, top and bottom. If it's up against a wall, ask to have it moved away so you can see the back. If the piece isn't too heavy, also ask the sales clerk to tip it over. Back panels should be inset and screwed into the frame. Those that are only tacked or stapled are not of high quality. In the best-made furniture, back and undersides are sanded and stained with a color; sometimes, they're even finished.

All movable parts should move smoothly: Pull out drawers, by the corners as well as the handles, and open and close doors. Drawers should have center and side guides and may have stops.

Check to see how the corners are joined. Mortise and tenon, dovetail, tongue and groove, or double dowel joints are sturdy and indicate good quality. Butt joints will wobble and pull apart in time. On heavier furniture, corner blocks should be in place, and all joints should be glued, then nailed or screwed together. (Large pieces should also have casters so you can move them easily.)

Give the furniture a heft test. Press your weight—all of it—against the side. If the piece twists, it's not solidly put together.

On metal furniture, joints should be smooth and carefully welded. Wicker and rattan furniture should have secure joints and no ragged edges.

Inspect dining tables in the same way for solid joints and sound construction. Then picture a party. Could you seat enough guests around the table, or would someone have to battle with a table leg? Sit on one of the dining chairs and wiggle about. Does it wobble, squeak, or creak? Is the chair comfortable to sit on?

Modular units are highly flexible. They're made to fit together or stack in a variety of shapes and in rooms of different sizes. All the units should be snug against each other. If you're placing modules on top of each other, check to see how they stack up. The top sections must hold firmly in place. (For more information on modular furniture, see pages 72 and 73.)

Finally, look at the grain of the wood. The top, sides, front, and legs of the furniture should be in the same tone. In addition, the grain should appear to flow from one part of the piece to another.

The inside storage

The interiors of many case goods pieces are especially designed to hold certain items. With the more flexible units, you can move the shelves up or down, or remove them completely.

Before selecting a piece, be sure you have a clear idea of what you need to store in it. There's no sense in buying furniture that can't hold its own as a storage unit.

For example, do you need many drawers or just a few? Pigeonholes may do, or perhaps you just want a simple

writing table where you can spread out and get down to business.

Choosing a bedroom chest also depends on the shape of things going into it. You may need only a few deep drawers to store blankets, bedding, and bulky clothing. On the other hand, if you're putting away lingerie, jewelry, and accessories, several shallow drawers may be better.

The line on finishes
The best wood furniture is finished by hand, but machine-finishing is also used on quality pieces. However the finish is achieved, tabletops, cabinet fronts, carved and molded parts should all look and feel smooth. If you see small bumps or ridges, the furniture was not rubbed well. In addition, the inside of cabinet doors should feel as smooth as the outside.

Some wood looks "distressed," but that may be a good sign. Distressing is a finishing process used to make furniture appear old by the addition of simulated scars and insect holes. But the distressed finish may indeed be distressing if the marks *look* as though they were mechanically done, rather than naturally resulting from old age.

The finish itself may be any number of substances—lacquer, varnish, oil, or plastic. (For more on finishing materials, see pages 74 and 75.)

Plastic laminates—plastic sheets that are bonded to the surface of a piece of furniture—resist heat, stains, moisture, and grease. However, they can be scarred, dented, and cut; caustic cleaners may also damage them.

Examine a laminated top as you would one of pure wood. The laminate will only be as smooth as the material under it: Lots of small bumps and scratches indicate poor workmanship. In addition, a good laminated top has a soft sheen, the result of rubbing it by hand with pumice.

The hard truth
Make sure to check the hardware on a piece of furniture; it has two purposes. Aesthetically, furniture hardware should complement the piece without overpowering it. Functionally, it should allow you to open and close all movable parts with a minimum of effort.

Brass is a popular hardware choice for high-quality, traditional-style furniture, although other materials may be used if they're consistent with a particular style. On less expensive pieces, you'll often find painted or brass-plated hardware, which looks good at first but may fade later on.

Feel it. If the hardware is metal, it will appear to be heavy. Pulls made of two connected parts should be securely put together. There should be piano hinges on drop-leaf desks, tables, and any piece with long heavy doors. Finally, make sure all metal trim is neat and solidly attached.

EVERY LABEL TELLS A STORY

Labels and hangtags can be an invaluable source of information about materials. Here's a guide to some of the more common terms you'll encounter.

• *Softwoods* come from trees like pine, cedar, and cypress that keep their foliage all year long. Softwoods are typically used in inexpensive and unfinished furniture. (See pages 74 and 75.)

• *Hardwoods* come from trees that lose their leaves every year, like walnut, oak, and chestnut; hardwoods are denser and stronger for their weight (but not necessarily "harder") than softwoods. Hardwoods tend to have richer grains and are used in fine furniture, usually as veneers.

• *Veneers*. Don't let your grandmother tell you that veneered wood is inferior. Fifty years ago, she was probably right. At that time, veneered wood was made by gluing a thin panel of exquisitely grained wood over a single layer of less expensive wood. In humid weather, the wood pieces alternately expanded and contracted, causing ugly warping. Also, the veneer itself tended to peel off. But now, the problems have been solved. New and more powerful glues prevent peeling, and new ways of putting wood together prevent warping. Panels are made by bonding several sheets of wood together, not just two, with the grains running in alternating directions (the middle piece is usually thicker than the others). Consequently, the entire panel remains stable without warping. In furniture made today, most of the large, flat surfaces, such as tops, sides, and cabinet doors, are veneered, as are the curved fronts of cabinets. Legs and framework are solid wood, however.

• *Solid* means that all exposed surfaces (tops, side panels, and drawer fronts) are made of the solid wood named on the tag—without veneer. However, wood on the inside of the furniture may be different from that on the outside.

• *Genuine*, used with the name of a particular wood —oak, for instance—means all exposed parts of the furniture are made of oak veneer over plywood.

• *Combination* means that exposed parts of the piece are made of more than one type of wood. Genuine walnut veneers, for example, might make up all exposed panels (except for inlays and accents), with numerous solid hardwoods forming the exposed solid parts.

• *All-wood construction* is a term meaning that all exposed parts are made of wood for the full thickness of the panel. Some manufacturers skimp by gluing a thin layer of wood to a wood frame, giving it the appearance of thick wood from the outside. Test for yourself by thumping the panel. Genuine wood gives a dead sound; a thin panel echoes.

Unlabeled furniture isn't necessarily a sign of poor quality. It's just up to you to find additional information about it.

WICKER, RATTAN, & OTHER CASUAL FURNITURE

There was a time when wicker furniture meant large Victorian porches, where people sat comfortably as they sipped mint juleps in the late afternoon sun. Rattan—if anybody knew the name—was deliciously curvy furniture that seemed to appear only in the steamy Oriental bars of countless World War II movies. How times have changed! Today, both wicker and rattan (along with similar materials) rank high on the list of valuable, versatile, and beautiful furniture for almost any environment.

As the natural look becomes a traditional favorite, few other furniture pieces fit in as easily as wicker and rattan. Crafted from various woody vines, they are compatible with plants, pottery, brick, stone, and other materials used to bring the outdoors inside.

On the other hand, while wicker and rattan are usually part of casual and relaxed settings—perfect for lounging in the afternoon—each can play a more sophisticated role in your decorating scheme. Painted or glazed and fitted with cushions of an elegant, high-fashion fabric, wicker and rattan pieces can match pedigree with even the most stately Chippendale chair or Queen Anne table. In fact, they're compatible with almost any furniture or decorating style.

Pieces of rattan and wicker have other things going for them besides their good looks. They were originally made to be lounged on and enjoyed. Whatever the style, they're still *comfortable.*

Quality wicker and rattan make sensible buys, too. Although most new furniture has little resale value, this isn't true with antique wicker or rattan pieces. Their unchanging appeal is a highly marketable quality—you get back close to what you paid for them. Because they're usually hand-crafted, they're notches above run-of-the-mill furniture. And because their character hasn't changed much over the years—and probably won't in the future—the investment is more than worth it.

Material differences

To many people, rattan, cane, wicker, and bamboo are one and the same. They're not.

Before you begin shopping, it's a good idea to know the general characteristics of each material.

• *Rattan* is a woody vine that's a member of the palm family. It can be shaped into a multiplicity of forms and, unlike bamboo, which is hollow, rattan doesn't split when bent and nailed. Growing free, it's a parasitic vine that can reach lengths of 500 feet. Before rattan is made into furniture, the outer bark is stripped off. The bark, or peel, is then cut into narrow strips and is often used to wrap the framework and joints of rattan pole furniture.

• *Cane* is even thinner strips, split from rattan's outer bark. It is woven into chair seats and furniture side panels, as well as accessory pieces.

• *Wicker* is a broad term that refers to any number of "woven" furniture pieces or accessories. Thus, wicker can be made from reed (segments of rattan's inner core), dwarf rattan, willow twigs, or nearly any other flexible vine.

However, wicker woven from the inner core of rattan is stronger and less brittle than that made of other materials. Even so, wicker of this kind doesn't have an outer bark to protect it, as dwarf rattan or willow twigs do, so it needs to be lacquered or varnished.

The weaves themselves are wonderfully varied and range from fine overall patterns to heavily textured or intricately woven designs.

• *Bamboo* looks like rattan, but it is hollow and has a tough outer shell, which makes it less

flexible than rattan. It is more difficult to shape, splits easily, and doesn't take a finish well.

• *Buri* and *raffia* are two other materials used in woven furniture. Buri is the spine or center stem of the palm leaf and is used most often to create lacy peacock or fan-backed chairs. Raffia comes from the leafstalks of the raffia-palm, as well as other trees and plants (banana, for example).

• *Willow* is, of course, a common tree or shrub with tough, malleable shoots. It's a long-lasting furniture material because it retains its natural moisture well. Willow is often used to make the rustic "twig" furniture that is again so popular today.

Furniture made from all of these materials—but especially wicker and rattan—is becoming increasingly popular with homeowners. The selection of styles and pieces is large. You can still find the old reliable rockers, love seats, coat and umbrella stands, and ferneries. But you'll also see new and practical items like bar carts, wine racks, Parsons tables, lamp tables, and étagères. In addition, manufacturers are combining rattan and wicker with chrome, glass, and plastic laminates. Finally, the materials come in natural finishes, lacquers, and antique glazes.

How to judge quality

Rattan furniture should be made of smooth, unblemished poles, each with similar dimensions. (Dark spots may indicate rotting.) In quality rattan, growth marks are the same size and approximately 12 to 18 inches apart.

Check the wrapping around each joint to see that it is even, neat, and tight enough so it won't slip or move when you pull your fingers across it. Any screws should be recessed. In quality pieces, round rattan moldings that edge a tabletop or other surface are applied with mitered corners. The molding should be glued and fastened in place and the fasteners countersunk.

The frames of rattan and wicker furniture determine how durable and comfortable the pieces are. Test each in the following ways:

When inspecting a chair, lean on it with all your weight. The frame should be strong and rigid and at least 1 inch thick. Now check the platform of the seating piece. Because all major parts are attached to it, the platform must be strong, preferably made of hardwood. Lift off the seat cushions to see how they're supported (the best have rubber straps for added strength). Find out, too, if the cover fabric is stain-resistant. Then put the cushions back and sit down. Are you comfortable?

Like the chairs, rattan and wicker tables must be rigid. Test them in the same way. Tabletops may be glass, laminated plastic, or wood. Each should be free of flaws and fitted solidly to the table.

Finally, check the finish. Wicker is often protected with a coat of polyurethane or varnish.

Treat it right

Except for regular dusting, rattan and wicker furniture need little help. (Dusting is easier if you use the vacuum's soft brush to get into the wicker weave.)

If the furniture has become badly soiled, use water and a mild soap solution. Accidental chipping poses no problem, either. Simply sand the area lightly, and apply the original finish.

If you have a piece of old wicker furniture, you can make it look colorfully new, like the one illustrated *at right*. Lightly sand the piece with medium-weight paper. Vacuum, then seal the wicker with a coat of flat-white primer paint, using a dabbing motion to sink the paint into the weave. Let the primer dry overnight, and finish it off with a coat of color.

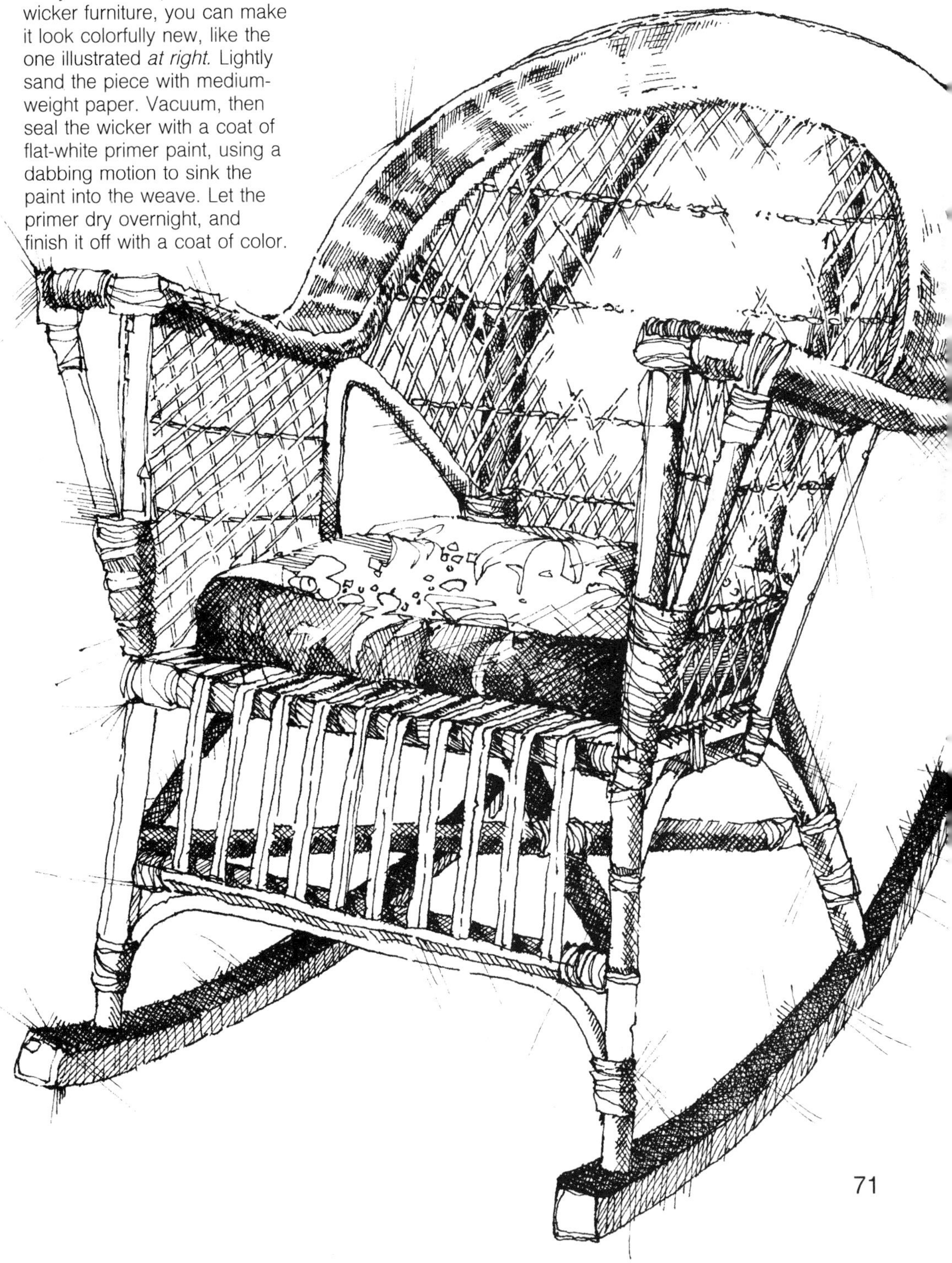

MODULAR & STORAGE PIECES

In the old days, most people placed a piece of furniture in one particular spot, and it would rarely stray from there. Years ago, modular seating was totally square in shape, contemporary in design, and large in scale. Today, however, you can find traditional and transitional styles, with gently curving frames and wood or metal trim. And because houses—and the rooms in them—continue to shrink in size, new modulars are often compact and smaller-scaled.

Modular flexibility allows you to stack or bunch seating pieces like building blocks. Individual pieces are as various as they are versatile. You should be able to easily find a choice array of modular armless sections, corner sections, end sections, and ottomans. Fitting them in is the only real problem. The trickiest part of selecting modulars is planning the number and kind of units your particular room can accommodate. Probably the best way to handle the problem is by drawing the room to scale and experimenting with paper cutouts of the units you intend to use.

Modular seating doesn't only make an impossible floor plan easier to cope with, it also means that you're never stuck

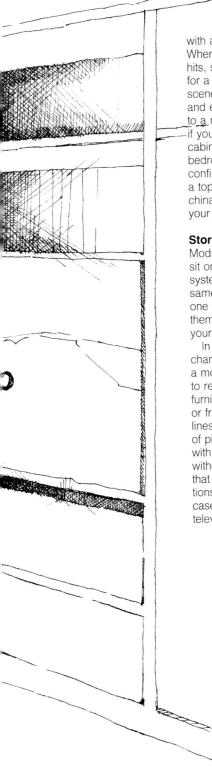

with a permanent arrangement. When the redecorating urge hits, simply regroup the pieces for a refreshing change of scene, or move them quickly and easily to another room—or to a new home. For example, if you're using a modular base cabinet as a dresser in your bedroom, there's no reason to confine it to one spot. Just add a top, and you have a new china cabinet, ready for use in your dining room.

Storage that won't stop

Modulars aren't made only to sit on. A modular storage system provides you with the same kind of flexibility—from one unit to a whole wall of them. Simply add pieces as your needs and budget grow.

In addition to giving you the chance to expand practically, a modular system allows you to rearrange your storage furniture from room to room or from home to home. Most lines have a varied selection of pieces, including cabinets with doors, open units with or without shelves, and pieces that take care of special functions—a desk, bar, or storage case for a stereo system or a television set.

Not only can you satisfy your basic storage needs, you can also find a diverse selection of special modular options: doors, drawers, shelves, light bridges, flip-down tables, and other kinds of furniture. You can even find a place to store the bed you sleep on, *opposite*.

Storage pieces are available in two standard depths, each with its own particular advantages. Wall modules that are 15 inches deep do best as hideaways for paraphernalia in the living room or dining room (books, tableware, accessories, etc.). Larger pieces —with a depth of 18 inches— are usually needed to store electronic gear and clothing.

There's nothing standard, however, about all the conveniences that storage modules can provide. For example, they may have recessed lighting, knockout holes for electrical wires, special water-resistant surfaces that make tending a bar easy, and pullout shelves for television sets and stereo systems.

Many modular storage systems have finished fronts and backs, so you don't have to bump them up against a wall. You can place pieces perpendicular to the wall or use one or more as freestanding room dividers. The flexible arrangement may improve traffic flow, save wall space, and organize your storage all at once.

Buy flexibly

Even more than most furniture, modular pieces need to be durable. Because you may give them a host of different jobs to do over the years, you should expect that they'll be around to perform.

Before buying, determine how you will use a piece. Remember that too much versatility may mean that furniture does 20 things satisfactorily but not one exceptionally well.

Select reliable brands and patronize reputable dealers. There, inspect the furniture as you would any other. Modular units should fit firmly together (especially if you plan to stack them). The backs of chairs and sofas shouldn't give when you stretch out on them. Pick fabrics you can afford and that are made of materials that fit your family. If the piece is destined for a lot of punishment, consider stain-resistant fabrics and dark colors that hide dirt better. Make sure patterns match and seams are tightly stitched.

UNFINISHED FURNITURE

Unfinished, factory-made furniture has been on the market more than 60 years, but for most of that time, the selection was woefully small and the furniture decidedly flimsy. In recent years, however, much unfinished furniture has proved to be a symphony of choices and value. In fact, many good raw-wood pieces are the equal of their finished counterparts in every way but one: You have to finish the job. But today the work isn't burdensome. If you're willing to do it, buying unfinished furniture may be the best deal you'll ever make.

Unfinished furniture now comes in almost every available type, from four-poster beds to Boston rockers. With some exceptions, most are put together well. There for the choosing are old-fashioned rolltop desks; high chairs and toy chests; desk/buffet combos that convert into tables; and a multitude of shelves, chests, and bookcases in a wide variety of sizes and prices.

You'll save money, no doubt about that. In fact, you should expect to pay about half of the price for a comparable finished piece of furniture.

Of course, some unfinished furniture is more expensive, although high-priced pieces can't be found in all parts of the country. Usually, the more costly items are reproductions or adaptations of period pieces, made with fine hardwoods and assembled with top-of-the-line craftsmanship. Early American, eighteenth-century English and French, and contemporary styles are readily available in all price ranges.

Whatever the size of your budget—big, small, or in between—you can find a diverse selection of appropriately nostalgic items like washstands, dry sinks, replicas of old spice chests, old-fashioned rockers, and classic bentwood and pressed wood chairs.

Where can you find this bonanza? Generally, you'll find the greatest variety, as well as the more expensive, quality lines, in specialty stores which sell only unfinished furniture. Lumberyards also sell a good deal of unfinished furniture, as do some department stores and major mail-order houses (check their catalogs). As a rule, however, more expensive lines are sold only in specialty stores or by mail order.

Get a piece of the action

Most unfinished furniture is made of either pine or oak, although other woods like cherry and walnut also are used for some higher-priced pieces.

Items with lower price tags are ordinarily made of clear, soft pine, with a little graining for added interest. Lodgepole or knotty pine, which is tougher, harder, and has a distinctively rustic look, is generally more expensive.

Quality hardwood furniture features dovetailed construction, with frames blocked and glued. Doors, drawers, and sides are all made of wood. Drawers have center guides, and cabinet doors hang true on their hinges.

The drawers of many inexpensive pieces are stapled together, and the bottoms and sides are usually made of fiberboard. Frames are nailed together.

If you're a competent do-it-yourselfer, you can assemble some unfinished furniture. Putting the pieces together on your own may save about $10 per item.

In most unfinished furniture, your choice is limited to colonial-style brass-plated drawer handles and door pulls, and small wooden knobs shaped like buttons. Corner brackets on campaign-style furniture are often plated with brass. But you don't have to stick with the standard hardware. With a little work, you can replace the originals with other pulls and hinges.

Wherever you decide to buy unfinished furniture, check for guarantees. Better lines carry limited warranties against defective workmanship and materials. If you get a piece with flaws, it will be repaired or replaced at no extra cost.

Finishing touches

Fortunately, finishing materials are not expensive; you can afford to buy the best. Even a large table or chest won't require enough finish to add significantly to the cost.

Be sure to work in a room with no drafts, and place a plastic drop cloth beneath the whole project to protect the floor.

The first step before applying the finish is sanding—hard, but necessary, work. Although unfinished furniture is sanded at the factory, you'll almost always have to do more yourself at home. How much more you do depends, obviously, on the condition of the furniture.

When you're done sanding, remove dust and other residue as thoroughly as possible. Using a piece of cheesecloth dampened with mineral spirits, wipe the surface completely.

Now you're ready to finish the job, but with what?

• *Stains* are really different kinds of wood dyes—penetrating oil and aniline dye powder mixed with denatured alcohol or water—and sealer and varnish stains, which are simply combined with the sealer or varnish.

Test any stain first by applying a small amount of the stain to an inconspicuous part of the furniture. Usually, the longer the stain stays on, the darker the final color will be.

Unfinished pine takes an even stain in almost any tone —fruitwood, maple, cherry, walnut, or mahogany. Of course, the graining won't be the same as in the wood you're trying to match, but the color will be.

Pine needs only a light sanding with fine sandpaper. The edges on less expensive pieces may be sharp, and the soft wood may nick and dent. If so, round the sharp edges just a little by first sanding lightly across the grain and then with the grain.

Maple is another story. It's so hard and dense that it won't absorb much stain. To open up the surface of the wood so more finish can sink in, give maple a very hard sanding.

For a look at stains and their effect on various woods, see pages 92 and 93.

• *Filler* is a smoother that's rubbed into the pores of wood to even out the surface. Unless you prefer the rough look, coarse-grained woods like oak need a filler. Most other woods used to make unfinished furniture don't need to be filled.

• *Sealers* are applied either before or after staining, depending on the manufacturer's directions. Sealers prevent fillers and stains from bleeding through to the finish coat.

• *Shellac* can either be a sealer or a finish, although as a finish it's not very durable. If you do use shellac as a finish, apply it with cheesecloth instead of with a brush. Let it dry thoroughly, then rub with fine steel wool, going with the grain, *never* across it.

• *Varnish* and *polyurethane* wear well—they both produce smooth, hard finishes.

• *Lacquer* dries more quickly than varnish but won't wear as well. Even so, it allows you to preserve the look of bare wood.

• *Linseed oil* is a good choice if you're looking for a mellow, old-fashioned appearance. For a durable finish, apply two or three coats of shellac, topped off by two or three rubdowns of the oil itself.

• *Wax* provides a lovely natural finish, but don't rub it into bare wood. Always apply wax over a sealer.

Apply here

All finishes wear best if you apply several thin coats, rather than one thick one.

If you're using varnish, shellac, or lacquer, cover about one-third of the brush with the finish. Tap the brush lightly to remove excess liquid, then gently brush the finish onto the surface of the wood, using just the tip of the bristles. *Always* brush in the direction of the grain.

After each coat of varnish or shellac is completely dry, smooth it with fine sandpaper or steel wool. Lacquer is the only clear finish that doesn't need sanding between coats.

QUICK-ASSEMBLY

It goes by many names —quick-assembly, lifestyle, easy-assembly— but they all add up to one thing: furniture you put together yourself. Although quick-assembly pieces are not available in every part of the country, their acceptance is growing rapidly. In any case, they really *are* easy to assemble, and, compared to conventional furniture, their price is economical. Here's what you need to know before you order cartons of your favorite furniture.

Easy-assembly furniture includes chairs, sofas, tables, cabinets, chests, and étagères you buy off the shelf and carry home in a carton. Because *you* put the pieces together, there's no time between the purchase and the delivery. In fact, if your car is large enough, you can pack it full of quick-assembly furniture that will fill an entire room or small apartment—and assemble it all in one day.

Although selling furniture in a box is not a new development (some stores have been retailing quick-assembly designs for more than a decade) the quality of these pieces has improved considerably in recent years. At the same time, the number and choice of styles have expanded rapidly, with more than 100 lines of living room, dining room, and bedroom furniture available.

As you may guess, prices are low—sometimes very low. Because quick-assembly furniture is less costly to produce, ship, and deliver, the manufacturer's savings land right in your pocket. Quick-assembly pieces carry price tags that are generally at least 20 percent lower than more conventional furniture. Occasionally, you'll find items up to 40 percent less expensive than similar goods assembled in a factory.

Like other kinds of furniture, some quick-assembly pieces are well designed and carefully constructed; others are money-savers that really aren't meant to last for years. In any event, most lines are well styled and serviceable.

Materials used to construct this furniture are common and easy to handle. They include wood, plastic, fiberboard, and chrome-finished steel or wrought iron. Some may have accents of rush, cane, or woven reeds. In most cases,

you'll need only a screwdriver and a hammer to assemble the whole thing. Some helpful manufacturers even include a screwdriver in the carton.

Changing styles
Simplicity is the order of the day. Most quick-assembly furniture is contemporary and clean-lined, with little ornamentation and hardware. Natural good looks—wood grains and textured fabrics—dominate. You can also find some Early American pieces, but many look more ruggedly western.

Where does this type of furniture fit in best? High-quality lines with wood frames and, believe it or not, some molded plastic pieces blend in easily in even the most sophisticated settings.

Furniture with a rustic look— knotty pine, for example— stands up well in a family room or first apartment. And all easy-assembly furniture offers an economical and tempting way to fill up a vacation home.

Putting pieces together
Different styles of upholstered furniture go together in different ways. Metal and wood frames are usually screwed or bolted together. In other styles, plastic or chrome pipes fit in place to form the framework. Still other pieces are held by metal hooks that fit over pins in a slot, or by wooden pegs pounded into holes that are drilled at the factory. Side panels slide into grooves in the frame or screw into position.

All the hardware should be part of the package, as should detailed instructions on how to put everything together. For that reason, open the carton soon after you bring it home, even if you're not going to assemble the furniture right away. Check to see that the instructions are there, along

with the correct number of connectors. Top-quality lines should have everything in place; occasionally, the less expensive furniture lines will have missing parts.

Buying tips— upholstered furniture
To judge easy-assembly furniture pieces in the store, you have to change the way you look at things. Because they're not standard furnishings, most don't have hardwood frames; even in the best of lines, they're made of pine, fiberboard, or woven reed or cane. Some pieces may have sides upholstered with the same fabric used on the cushions.

Regardless of the material, any framework should be rock solid. Samples of the furniture should be there for the touching. Ask if you can take a piece apart and put it back together. After all, it should really *be* easy to assemble.

Sit down on sofas and chairs. They should be as stable as conventional furniture, with no creaking or squeaking. If the piece feels flimsy, it probably *is* flimsy and will fall apart as easily as you put it together.

If the frames are chrome, iron, or metal, all exposed surfaces should be electrostatically finished to protect them against chipping and peeling.

The upholstery itself should not be second-rate, either. Check the tailoring. Fabric patterns should match, as they do on conventional furniture, and be centered on the back and seat cushions.

In most of these lines, cushions are not made with welts (boxed and welted cushions are more expensive to produce). Nor do many sofas have springs. Ordinarily, the cushions rest on a box base or on a length of fabric slung between the top back and bottom front rails of the piece.

For these reasons, fabric slings and cushions should be reinforced with interlinings. The parts that will support weight should be double stitched to provide added strength. (For more details on the makeup of upholstered furniture, see pages 64-66.)

**Buying tips—
case goods**
Cabinets, étagères, and tables come together in much the same way as easy-assembly chairs and sofas. (Relatively few manufacturers make beds, dining tables with chairs, or

chests of drawers. Most quick-assembly lines do include end tables and cocktail tables to match sofas and chairs.)

As you would with pre-assembled furniture, carefully check the construction. Are edges tight, with no cracks? Are surfaces smooth and carefully finished? Are tables stable and sturdy? Do modular units fit together firmly?

In easy-assembly lines, most of the shelving units stand on the floor, although a few are meant to hang on the wall.

Be sure that the shelves have sturdy brackets that will support a heavy load. Open and close doors on cabinet display models. Do they fit well and open smoothly? Check all the drawers. While you probably won't find dust panels or center guides, quality quick-assembly furniture should have side guides so the drawers will move smoothly.

Test the tables by jiggling them. Do they feel stable? Do they feel sturdy enough to support some weight, such as a stack of books? If there is a glass top, is it tempered glass that will not break or crack easily? For more information on the makeup of case goods, see pages 67-69.

77

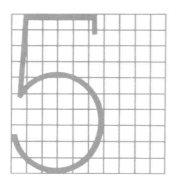

CREATING BUILT-IN STORAGE

Are your family centers afflicted by a storage shortage? A capacious built-in can solve the problem efficiently and economically. Best of all, you can make one to order, creating a unit that—like a well-tailored suit—fits your own special needs. But be warned that a project like this is a permanent addition to your home, so creating a well-thought-out plan is vitally important. This chapter will help. It describes, in step-by-step detail, how to go about planning, designing, and building a built-in family entertainment center. Chapter 6 tells how to create modular seating; Chapter 9 shows examples of other projects that you can build.

SIZE UP THE AVAILABLE SPACE

As the descriptions on the opposite page make clear, built-ins are beautifully flexible; they'll fit almost anywhere and serve a variety of functions. But the secret to successful building is a rather *in*flexible one: knowing exactly how much room you have to work with.

Once you've selected a wall, make a rough sketch of it, including the locations of electrical and heating outlets, pipes, windows and window casings, doors and door swings, and other features that may enter into the design. Don't worry about precision at this point. The idea here is to get a rough drawing on which you can record measurements.

Then start measuring (a retractable metal tape, with a friend holding one end, works best). Measure the wall—precisely, now—at the top, middle, and bottom. Also, note the widths of the door and window openings and the distances between them. As you take a measurement, clearly mark it on the sketch. When you're through, repeat the process, double-checking the accuracy of each distance. In addition, make sure the wall and adjoining walls are plumb. If they aren't, plan to shim.

Remember one thing as you're working: These measurements must be extremely accurate. If they're not, you'll pay for the mistakes later.

TYPICAL HEIGHT DIMENSIONS

Paperback books	8″
Hardback books	11″
Catalog-format books	15½″
Record albums	13¼″
8-track tapes	6¼″
Cassette tapes	5″
Circular slide trays	9¾″

FOUR PLACES TO PUT WALL UNITS

Built-ins can fit in nearly anywhere in your home. Try building simple open shelves for the kitchen or a long storage wall for the family room or a built-in unit around the fireplace—every room has possibilities, waiting to be exploited.

To illustrate the various options open to you, we've drawn up the room shown here and outfitted it with four different hypothetical built-ins. It's unlikely that you'd choose to construct all of them in any one room, but you just may spot a location you haven't thought of.

1 Many homes have no separate dining rooms. A divider wall can define a separate eating area and still maintain a feeling of openness. In this sketch, cabinets below provide storage, a pass-through counter makes serving easy, and open shelves above are accessible from either side of the unit.

2 It's easy to overlook a wall with windows, doors, or other architectural elements, yet adding built-ins to this outside wall helps to unify the entire room. Open shelves and cabinets put the wall to work. Before the built-ins were added, this wall was a challenge to furniture arrangement.

3 Turn a long, empty wall into the focal point of a room with a well-planned storage/entertainment center. Books, records, a television set, and stereo equipment all find a home in this arrangement.

4 A fireplace often divides a wall in two, making it hard to use the space productively. Built-in shelves can rescue the lost space and put it to good use for storage and display.

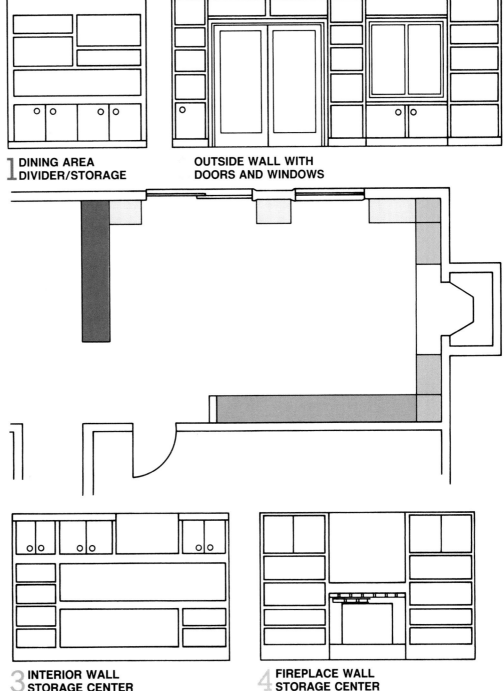

1 DINING AREA DIVIDER/STORAGE

OUTSIDE WALL WITH DOORS AND WINDOWS

3 INTERIOR WALL STORAGE CENTER

4 FIREPLACE WALL STORAGE CENTER

MAKE FINISHED DRAWINGS

1

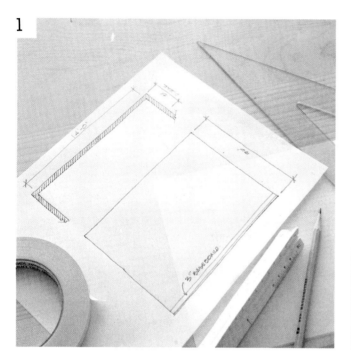

2

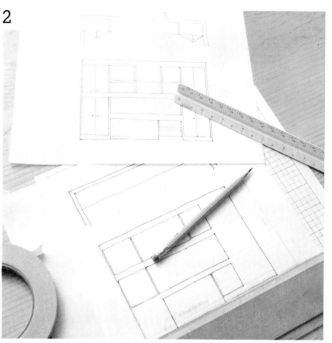

5

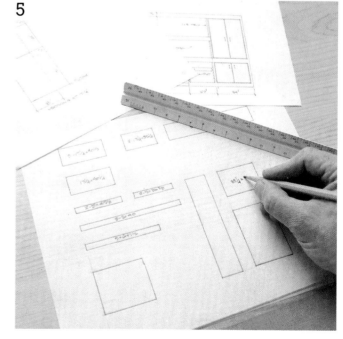

Once you have a line on the space available, it's time to transform your rough sketch into a finished, meticulously scaled mechanical drawing. A mechanical is simply what the name implies —a drawing done with the help of instruments, rather than freehand.

The mechanical equipment you'll need to complete your drawing appears in the photos on these two pages—a pen or sharp pencil, graph paper, tracing paper, masking tape, a clear plastic triangle, as well as an architect's scale. Ordinarily, a scale of ½ inch works best; if it fits your plans, buy graph paper with ½-inch squares.

Tape tracing paper over a piece of graph paper, and start drawing the wall. For example, to represent a 10-foot-long wall, draw a line 10 squares long. Use the architect's scale to double-check the counts you make on the graph paper.

For a project like this, you can make two kinds of finished drawings. In effect, the rough you sketched earlier is an *elevation* drawing, or *view,* which shows how a wall appears when you look at it straight on. If the wall has few, if any, features, a precisely rendered elevation is probably unnecessary. On the other hand, a *section* drawing, which represents interior details you can't see from the outside, may be indispensable. The concept isn't hard: Compare making a section view to sawing away part of a wooden box and peering inside.

No matter what the drawing, don't be afraid to experiment. Using a lot of inexpensive tracing paper at this stage is better than making much more expensive mistakes later on.

1 The rough sketch you did earlier must include exact measurements and structural features of the wall you have in mind.

2 Now make rough sketches of different arrangements, fitting them into the space available and designing them to meet your storage needs.

3 Transform the plan for the unit into a finished, scale drawing. The larger the scale, the more detail you can include in your drawing.

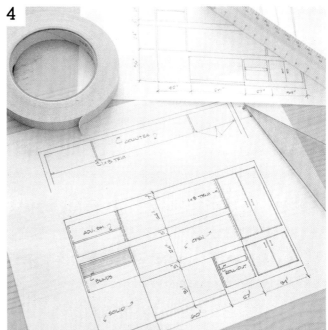

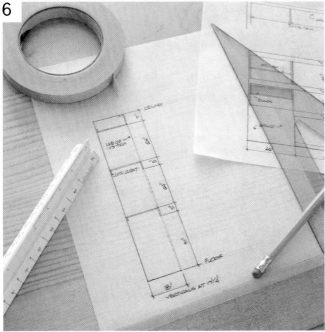

4 The finished elevation is a two-dimensional drawing of the unit, showing the height and width. The depth is indicated at the top of the sheet.

5 The finished section drawing also shows the depth of the unit. Make sections to show aspects not pictured on elevation or plan drawings.

6 Make a cutting diagram (see page 84) so you can determine how many materials, such as sheets of plywood, you will need.

7 Referring to the finished drawings, make a materials list and determine how much to order.

LAY OUT YOUR UNIT ON THE WALL

Now it's time to indulge yourself a little. With the design in mind and the drawings finished, use a pencil to mark out the entire project on the wall itself. Follow the plan, of course, but be flexible, too—this is your last chance to make changes before ordering materials and beginning construction of your built-in.

Clear the wall entirely, and move nearby furnishings so you can work without obstacles. Next, locate studs and mark their spacing on the wall; you'll attach ledgers to them when you're putting up the project. (Ledgers are horizontal strips of wood used to support the ends or edges of a project.) Generally, studs are either 16 or 24 inches apart. Start at the center of the wall, and rap along it with your knuckles. A solid *thunk* means you've found a stud. If rapping doesn't work, check the base-

board for nails. They're usually driven in at stud intervals. You may even want to use a special magnetic tool—called a stud finder—to zero in on nails or screws holding the surface of the wall to the studs.

Then, using a tape measure and a level, mark the exact location of each unit. This full-scale representation is like a dress rehearsal in more ways than one. Use the pencil drawing to make sure the items you plan to store actually will fit, that the scale is appropriate to the size of the room, and that the new built-in will not disrupt the flow of traffic in any way. If something isn't quite right, now's the time to tinker with the design.

MAP A
CUTTING
DIAGRAM

The design is on the wall, and you know it fits the assigned space. Before ordering materials, take one more step to make sure the project comes together as precisely as it should. Sketch out a simple but accurate model —called a cutting diagram— that shows how you'll cut the actual panels. This attention to detail, though not essential, is a good way to avoid wasting expensive materials later.

To make a cutting diagram, refer to your drawings. Working in ½-inch scale, cut out pieces of illustration board; they represent your 4x8-foot panels. Then cut pieces of kraft paper to represent the various sections making up the unit. Arrange the pieces on the illustration board until you find the most efficient way to use the material.

This built-in is cut from particleboard, but you could also work with either plywood or waferboard.

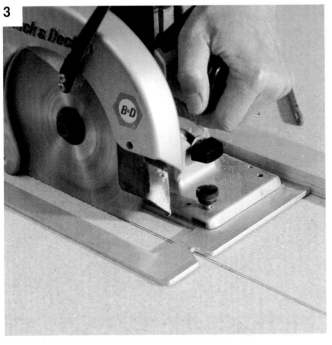

1 A cutting diagram substitutes scissors and paper for saw and particleboard. Use one to determine the best cutting pattern for your cabinet.

2 Then transfer your scale diagram to the actual panel, marking the cutting lines with a pencil and square.

3 Remember to allow ⅛ inch for the width of the saw kerf when you're laying out the pattern. Otherwise, the dimensions will be off.

4 Use a clamped straight-edge of milled 1x2 or 1x4 lumber or a metal carpenter's straightedge to guide a hand-held circular saw.

CONSTRUCT THE COMPONENTS

Assembling a built-in unit is a little like putting together a simple jigsaw puzzle. Any built-in is basically a series of boxes or boxlike components. The easiest way to assemble the components is to build them step by step (as you'd put together a puzzle piece by piece) and attach them to the wall afterward.

What tools do you need? You should have a power saw or handsaw, hammer, drill and screwdriver, plus some nails, glue, and sandpaper.

The sample project in this chapter—a series of boxes and shelves—is a family entertainment center designed to fit an entire wall (see page 89 for the impressive results). The two end storage boxes went together first, followed by the box shelves. The built-in also includes a special roll-out shelf

for the turntable, a shelf that glides easily into one of the end storage boxes.

All pieces are fastened with white glue and nails, then the rough edges are sanded.

Before attaching the pieces of the unit to the wall, you may have to remove any baseboard or ceiling moldings that are in the way. Use a pry bar and backsaw if needed.

There are a number of ways to attach built-ins, depending on the room and the style of the unit. A room divider, for example, will be attached at the floor and ceiling. In this sample project, the entire entertainment center is attached directly to the wall; some parts are supported on ledgers attached to the wall studs (more about this on page 88).

1

2

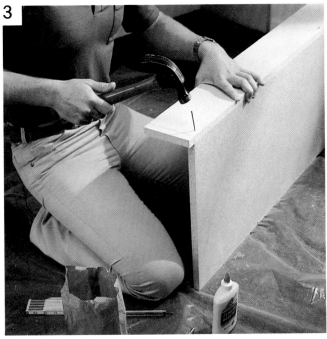

3

4

1 Remove the section of the baseboard where the bottom of the cabinet butts directly to the wall.

2 Each component must be horizontally level and vertically plumb. To keep them in position, clamp the units together as you work.

3 Build the shelves and attach the facing. Shelf units will rest on ledgers attached to the wall.

4 Measure the lip depth of the glide, and attach a 1x3 strip as a side rail for the roll-out drawer glide.

PUT IT ALL TOGETHER

The end is in sight! You're now ready to put everything together and attach it to the wall. If all your drawings and measurements have been accurate, the four final steps photographed and described on this page should lead you without a hitch to the finished project, *opposite.*

This built-in entertainment center is ideal for today's smaller homes. One wall-length unit could house an entire family's games, hobbies, and recreational equipment. In addition, it has places for a television set, stereo components, and a sewing center, plus room for a slide-away table and a collection display on the upper shelves. One other distinctive note: Stylish slimline blinds—not the same old doors—are an attractive way to close the shelves from view.

The unit is 18 inches deep, so it can accommodate the slide-away table. The overall length of the built-in is 14 feet.

The storage unit is made from ¾-inch particleboard and painted a warm peach color with a durable paint. But that's only one way to finish the job. For finishing alternatives, turn to pages 92 and 93. And to learn about planning and constructing seating modules like the ones next to our built-in wall unit, consult the following chapter.

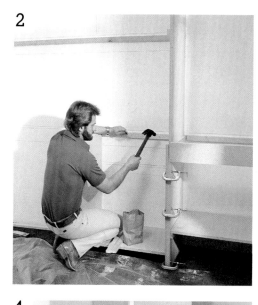

1 Use adjustable metal shelf clips to support the inside shelves. To position the clips correctly, drill holes 10 inches on-center. Make the job easier by using a ½-inch dowel as a drill stop.

2 Nail in ledgers so you can attach the desk-top counter and upper storage shelves to the wall. A 1x2 ledger is sufficient; position it on the wall in the location you marked out earlier. Again, check for level before securing the ledger to the wall.

3 The boxed shelf with facing lip (see page 87, photo 3) slips into place on the ledger. Nail it along the back, affixing it to the ledger and to the vertical side of the adjoining cabinet. Hold the units in place with C-clamps while you work.

4 Make the finishing touches —installing doors, for example—only after you've securely attached all the units to the wall and to each other. Doors must be shimmed and leveled to operate properly.

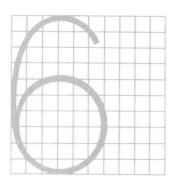

CREATING MODULAR SEATING

Maybe you've always wanted to have a hand in building your own furniture, but the intricacies of making it on your own have stopped you from starting. Not every project requires the touch of a master craftsman. If you'd like to learn how to build some easy-to-make furniture, have a seat for a few minutes and read this chapter. You'll find a step-by-step guide to planning and building a simple, attractive, and eminently comfortable modular sofa. After you've mastered these basics, take a look at pages 132-143 for some other furniture projects you can build.

THE BASICS OF FURNITURE DESIGN

Building simple, practical, and good-looking furniture isn't as difficult as you may think—but it does require some thought and a careful plan. If you want to put together seating pieces of any kind—chairs, sofas, love seats —keep the following in mind.

The size of it

Every *comfortable* seating piece—and comfort can be a visual as well as a physical quality—is sized to accommodate people in a particular setting. It should not only feel good to individuals of average size, but it should also fit into its surroundings without appearing to be too large or too small. The question is, what's a comfortable size?

To find the answer, first check out the territory. Where you intend to place the finished project will influence its size and shape. For example, in a den designed to serve only a few people, you should be able to build a piece using the *maximum* dimensions noted in the box on the opposite page. However, in an area set up to hold a small crowd—a family room, let's say—you may have to construct several pieces to the *minimum* dimensions. In the process, you sacrifice a bit of physical comfort for more seating.

One quick but effective way to pinpoint comfortable dimensions is to select a chair or sofa you already own and simply measure it (assuming, of course, it's not a lemon you wish you had never bought). Determine height, width, depth, and "kick space."

• *Height.* Measure from the floor to the top of the seat. When you're planning a unit, be sure to take into account the thickness of the cushion, if there is one. A 16-inch measurement, for example, may

be just 12 inches of structure and 4 inches of cushioning. Also measure from the floor to the top of the back and, on a piece with arms, from the floor to the top of the arm.

• *Width.* Ask a person to sit down, or more than one person if you're planning a sofa. Measure from leg side to leg side (or from buttock to buttock). For a chair, of course, you'll get a single measurement, but a sofa built to seat three will yield three identical numbers. If the piece has arms, measure their width as well (2½ inches is a comfortable distance).

• *Depth.* Measure from front to back. When planning, you can allow for a depth of up to 40 inches—but only if the piece has a back cushion; otherwise, 40 inches is probably too deep. (A normal back cushion is 3½ to 4 inches thick.)

• *Kick space,* or the area directly beneath a chair or sofa, is basically a design element, although it does make cleaning easier. Generally, this space will be no more than 3 inches high and 2 inches deep.

Measuring up

What do all your numbers show? Comfort. For example, a person of average size will sit comfortably on a sofa that's 17¾ inches high (from the floor to the top of the seat); 24 inches wide (per person); and 24 inches deep (29 inches on a sofa with a back).

Once you have an idea of comfortable sizes, it's time to build a project of your own. Beginning on page 92 are instructions on how to plan and build a simple modular sofa made from four boxes of identical size (along with a fifth that can be used as an ottoman).

SIZING SEATING

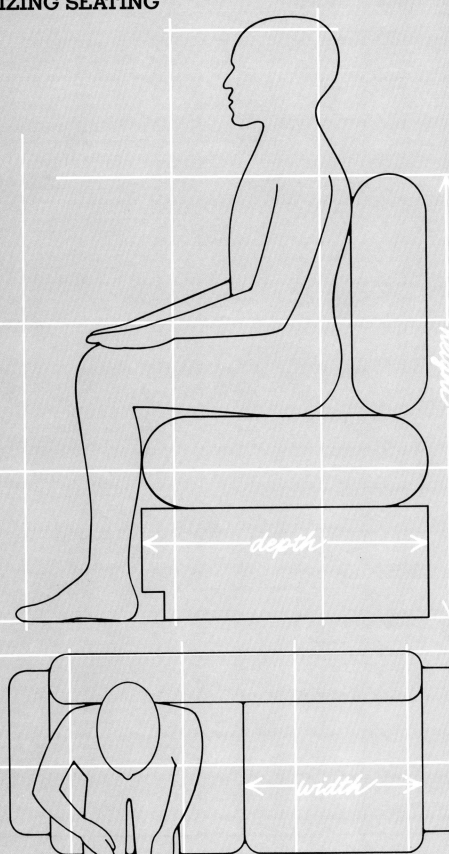

Although everyone has their own idea of the *perfectly* comfortable chair or sofa, certain measurements help to define a pleasant place to sit down. For the following dimensions, the first number indicates minimum size in inches; the second, maximum size; and the third, the most comfortable size for a person of average stature.

• *Height.* From floor to top of seat: 15, 19, 17¾ (including the thickness of cushions, if any). From floor to top of back: 27½, 34¼, 30½. For a piece with arms, from floor to top of arm: 24, 26, 25.

• *Width.* For a single unit, from leg side to leg side of a person sitting down: 18, 27, 24. Pieces designed to accommodate more than one person will be larger by a factor equal to the total number of units. To illustrate, the same widths for a three-unit sofa are 54, 81, 72.

• *Depth.* From front to back: 22½, 40, 29 (with a cushion or cushions 3½-5 inches deep). Without cushions, the maximum distance is 35 inches; the most comfortable, 24 inches.

• *Kick space.* From floor to bottom edge of the piece: 2½ to 3 inches. From the bottom edge of the piece to supports underneath the unit: 1¾ inches. (See page 96 for a photograph of a seating piece—one raised on a *plinth*, or base—with kick space built in.)

PLAN THE BOXES

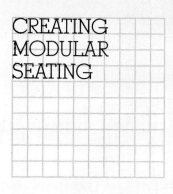

If you've never built furniture before, you may fear you'll end up with something you'd be reluctant to even *show* to friends and relatives, let alone ask them to sit on. This project, a series of modular cubes, is relatively easy to construct; it should be a good confidence-builder. Plus, you can apply the basic principles learned here to a variety of other projects.

It's a good idea to bone up a bit on elementary building skills before beginning a project so you don't waste time and money later on. Then, begin planning. Start by sizing up the room in which you'll put the sofa, making sure there's adequate space for the approximate dimensions you want. Next, choose the precise dimensions for each cube—they'll be the same—and for the project as a whole (see pages 90 and 91 for advice on how to determine the right size).

At this stage, too, think about the kind of furniture wood or plywood you intend to use. (Pages 154-157 explain how to select sheet goods and lumber.) Although you can, of course, choose solid wood, you may find that sheet goods such as plywood or particleboard are the best material to use. Either permits you to size the box more flexibly, which isn't the case when you're building with solid wood. This is because solid wood boards rarely measure more than 11½ inches wide; to achieve wider dimensions, you'd need to edge-join boards—a tricky process. Also, sheet goods' large size and factory-straight edges mean you make fewer cuts to get the same results.

Once you've settled upon the dimensions, use a pencil to make a rough sketch of the

A SEATING UNIT HAS MANY USES

Modular units are so flexible that you'd have a hard time *not* thinking of extra ways to use them.

As you'll see when you've finished this project, each box has an abundance of usable interior space. In this case, the instructions call for adding a drawer, which provides additional, convenient storage.

In fact, building seating modules that also serve as storage containers is the most common way to make them do double-duty. But using drawers is just one option; you can also construct a top that lifts off or one that's controlled by spring action. Sliding doors and cabinet doors are two other good alternatives. Of course, you can always leave the box open on one side and store items without closing them off in any way.

Unlike many other kinds of furniture, nearly all modular seating pieces are wonderfully mobile. You can rearrange the units at a moment's notice—using them as dividers, for instance—and completely change the appearance of a room.

Finally, each module can star in its own right. Detach one from a sofa, and you have a single seating piece, ottoman, or storage container.

entire sofa, and from that, a set of working drawings, complete with dimensions and cutting instructions. If you want to change sizes, do it now—dealing with a simple erasure at this point is far easier than trying to salvage miscut materials later on.

Next, compile a list of the materials you'll need. Note the wood and its size, along with any necessary building supplies (see the instructions on pages 96 and 97 to find out what's required).

When the materials are at hand or ordered, check to make sure you have all the right tools. Then, following your working drawings, measure and mark out the pieces to be cut. Do this carefully and slowly. An error common among beginners is cutting pieces too small, an expensive waste of wood.

Box tips
When the planning's over, you're ready to begin construction. But before you take the next steps—selecting a finish and actually building the boxes—note the following points about this most basic of all shapes.

• Plan cuts so the grain of the wood pieces runs the same way after the box is assembled. (Particleboard, of course, has no discernible grain.)

• After sawing, make sure that all edges are straight and each corner is square; otherwise, joints won't mate properly and the boxes may wobble.

SELECT
A FINISH

Shown *above* is a selection of sturdy materials for building the boxes. From top to bottom, they are: plastic laminate, oak veneer plywood, solid cherry, redwood, fir plywood, pine furniture blank, hardboard, and clear pine.

Once you've chosen the material, pick a finish. To check appearance, apply the paint or stain to the surface of a test piece— remember, of course, to experiment only with the material you'll use in building the boxes. (The man *at left* is testing paint on particleboard.) If you're not satisfied with the look, try other finishes, using the same piece.

The modular project on the next two pages has a paneled surface, and the photos *above*, from left to right, show three alternatives: *paint*, which gives you more flexibility in choosing colors and masks particleboard's mottled surface; *stain*, which often goes better with existing furniture, and works nicely on grained plywood; and *plastic laminate*, which is highly durable and easy to clean.

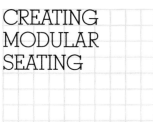
BUILD A SERIES OF BOXES

Follow these steps to construct one box that is made from particleboard and paneling:

1 Start the box by adding sides to a bottom. Butt-join all edges.

2 Build a top in the same way. To make sure the joints are solid, glue first, then nail them together with 6d finishing nails.

3 Now glue and nail on 1x2-inch trim to the front edges. The trim's raised surface forms a stop for the seat cushion and prevents it from sliding off.

4 Cut paneling to fit the surfaces, making sure you get a tight fit. Then apply with panel adhesive and, for extra stability, a few ring-shank nails. (You can, of course, use one of many other finishes at this stage. See pages 94 and 95 and *below*.)

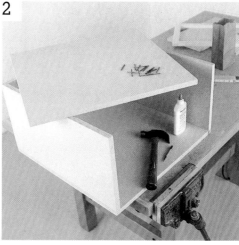

ALTERNATE BOX SURFACES

Particleboard and paneling are two solid choices for box surfaces. Here, from left to right, are three equally good surfaces (the first one is in a different motif, the other two are trimmed like the one above):
• a box finished in black plastic laminate and raised on a plinth, or base, for a sleek, out-of-the-ordinary visual effect;

• a box made of particleboard and painted, with screen molding applied for added detail;
• and a box constructed from a good face veneer plywood and then stained. If you choose a furniture-grade face veneer, use stain to finish.

5 Cover the paneling joints with wood corner angles; cut them long enough to over-lap the 1x2 trim.

6 Finish out the trim, making sure all butts are flush.

7 To construct the drawer, first determine the box's interior dimensions and subtract ⅛ inch from the top and sides. Then build another box, open on top; panel the exterior side, and slide it in. No drawer guides are necessary; to make sliding easier, run beeswax on the bottom of the drawer.

8 Complete the box by cutting out a hand pull. Center a rectangle, 2¼ inches wide and 1½ inches deep, on the face of the drawer's paneled side, scribing it with a square. Then drill holes at the top corners of the rectangle to allow cutting space for a saber saw. Finally, cut out the rectangle and smooth all the edges by sanding lightly.

5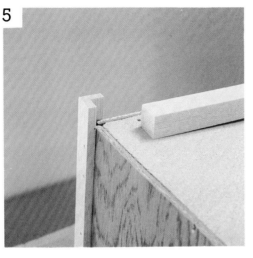

6

7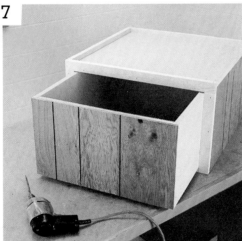

8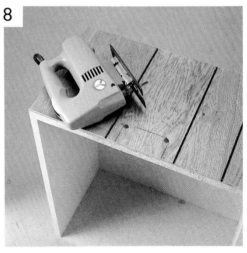

HOW TO MAKE CUSHIONS FOR THE FINISHED UNIT

The last step in creating a colorfully comfortable seating piece like the one shown *opposite* is upholstering cushions for it.

To begin, first select cushion forms sized to fit the boxes. The ones here are made of 4-inch, high-density foam, but you can buy ready-made "foam-rubber" forms in nearly any size, either molded or cut to specifications. You can also purchase forms made of shredded foam rubber, kapok, or synthetic fibers. Although these cushions have no casings, many store-bought forms

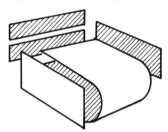

come with a muslin cover, which, if you want a casing, is the best material to use in any upholstering project.

If you like, you can even make your own forms, filling them with polyester fiberfill, shredded foam, kapok, or cotton batting. The latter is sold in a roll about 16 inches wide and 1 inch thick.

Then, to make the simple cushions pictured here, follow the instructions, *below.*

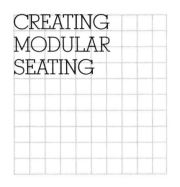

1 Make a paper pattern for five identical slipcovers; use the illustration, *above,* as a guide for laying the pattern pieces out around the forms. Be sure to allow at least a ½-inch seam allowance. Pin the pattern to the material, and cut the fabric, following its lengthwise and crosswise grains.

2 With right sides facing (wrong side out), stitch the seams of the left and right sides to the main piece. The main piece will need a small tuck at each of the front four corners so it will fit against the square sides. To reinforce your work, stitch ⅛ inch outside the original seam.

3 Sew a zipper the length of the cushion to the two back pieces. Still working with right sides together, sew the zippered back panel to the rest of the slipcover. Reinforce.

4 Turn the slipcover right side out; insert the foam. Zipper it shut. Repeat each step for the other slipcovers.

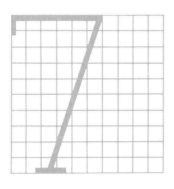

ROOMS FOR FUN & GAMES

How you spend your leisure time is important. For many of us, playing a game of pool, tending a greenhouse, picking out tunes on the piano, or turning over a high poker hand have always been relaxing ways to put a little fun into our lives. Today, sophisticated electronic games add a new dimension to our leisure time. But no matter how you spend your free time, where you spend it is equally important. To fit in all the fun you can, plan places for play that will provide the space and equipment that your indoor leisure activities require.

VIDEO CENTERS

Until recently, *video* simply meant a color or black-and-white television set in a console, tabletop, or portable case. Today, projection television sets, video games, video cassette recorders (VCR), video disc players, home video cameras, as well as other electronic devices, also compete for our viewing time, and for the space we allot to them. Most new video gear requires that you do more than simply sit and stare at a screen, so plan your family center so that you'll realize the maximum use of your video equipment.

First, ask yourself whether you want video to always play a dominant role in the room, or be hidden away when it's not in use. In the room shown *above*, a big-screen television set occupies center stage. Nearby, a VCR shares shelves with audio gear and a video game system; hand controllers extend to reach the seating in the foreground.

When space is tight

If you don't have space for a big, permanently displayed screen, select equipment that's less obtrusive, or plan built-ins to suit your video needs. Some big-screen systems come concealed in a cabinet; press a button and a motor lifts the screen out of the top. Other systems place the projection equipment in a small end-table-size cabinet, which you can use as a table when the television is off; simply open the cabinet and project onto a white wall or roll-up screen.

If you want to keep video gear totally out of the picture when it's not in use, custom built-ins are the ultimate way to go. In the room shown *opposite*, a special platform for the television set slides out of a wall cabinet and puts the set at the best viewing angle; slide the platform back into the cabinet and folding doors cover it up. A companion cabinet holds more video gear.

AUDIO
CENTERS

"How does this sound?" is one of the more common questions asked today. To ensure that your hi-fi components and speakers put out only the optimum quality of sound, first survey the room—aurally as well as visually—trying one speaker here and another one over there. Look and listen for that "hole-in-the-middle" spot where you are aware of two very separate and distinct sources of sound, with no blending of those sounds coming from the speakers. Should your survey turn up the perfect spot, but the dimensions seem all wrong, don't despair. New speakers are now available to fit almost any space.

Where you put the speakers is the most important decision you'll make in arranging your audio center equipment; the other components can go almost anywhere, as long as you are able to reach them easily.

Although there is no one recommended distance to separate speakers, there is a limited *range* of distances for speakers to sound the way they should. To find out what distance works best in your room, try a test. Move the speakers apart until you are aware of two separate sound sources, with no blending of sounds coming from the speakers. This is called the "hole-in-the-middle" spot, the maximum distance you can keep between the speakers.

Sound frequencies produced by stereo speakers behave differently; keep the individual characteristics in mind when you're placing the speakers. *Middle* (or *midrange*) and *high frequencies* travel straight out of the speaker's face. But *lower* or *bass frequencies* radiate equally in all directions from the speaker cabinet.

Middle and high notes will sound better if you place the speakers as close to ear level as possible, aimed directly at the listening area. Once you do this, increase or decrease the bass or "booming" sound by moving the speakers in relation to the walls. If you move the speakers close to a hard-surfaced rear wall or corner, you'll get more bass because the lower frequencies radiating from the back of the speaker cabinet bounce off the wall. To tone down bass sounds, move speakers away from the wall or corner.

High-tech vs. high style

Although you can't see the speakers in the sound system *opposite*, they're in opposite corners of the same wall that holds the pictured gear shelf. And because the wall, like the floor, is covered with commercial carpet, the speakers are on stands, placed two feet from the corner. Their location cuts down on the absorption of bass notes by the soft walls and floor. To allow easy access to the system, the owner used high-tech industrial shelving and exposed wiring and lighting.

A more imaginative approach for arranging audio systems is to turn the components into high-tech art, like those in the room pictured at *upper right*. Framed in wood, most components are at eye level. The turntable stands alone as a piece of sculpture, resting atop a low record cabinet that runs the length of the wall. The room's winged walls direct sound from the speakers to the sitting area to make the sofa an ideal listening spot.

The owner of the system pictured *at lower right* took a traditionally integrated approach and placed the audio components on existing surfaces (in this case, built-in shelving). The components match the depth of the shelves and fit flush with the fireplace wall. In addition, the dark shelves match the speaker grilles, a happy combination that plays down the size of the speakers themselves.

MOVIES & SLIDES

Despite the electrifying growth of new video technology, slides and home movies are still the best ways to record your family's history. Both are less expensive and provide better images than their electronic counterparts. And when it comes to editing finished pictures, both are more versatile. Here are some tips for better viewing.

Don't show movies and slides on a white wall: you probably won't like the quality of the picture. You might try hanging a bed sheet or tablecloth on the wall, but, again, the quality of the picture will suffer unless you can stretch the fabric taut enough to eliminate all of the folds.

Obviously, the solution is to purchase a projection screen, especially because it's the least expensive component in a projection system. You have three types to choose from: the normal white screen, the crystal-beaded screen, and the daylight screen. Choose the normal white screen when viewers will sit off to its side, the beaded type when viewers will sit in front of the screen, and the daylight type when you can't completely darken the room.

Screen frames also differ. The best and most expensive kind is mounted permanently, either built into a ceiling, like the one *opposite*, or mounted in a box on a wall or ceiling. The stand-up screen, however, comes in a wider variety of sizes. Its adjustable legs allow you to put the screen directly in front of the projecter. (If you tilt the projector upward to hit a ceiling-mounted screen, you'll get a distorted image.)

When you're choosing a spot for the projector, think first about how large an image you'll want and where your family will be sitting in the room. Choose a spot farthest from the screen, but one with easy access to light switches. Also, try to keep projector cords from stretching across the room; in the dark, viewers may easily trip over them. The projector in the room shown *at right* fits into a storage compartment in the seating platform, which provides plenty of sprawling space.

NUMBERS TO KNOW

Typical screen sizes for movies and slides: 30x40 inches to 72x96 inches (for tripod and wall- or ceiling-mounted roll-up screens).

A 40-inch screen, the standard size used in homes, should be set up at a distance of 14 feet from the projector. The actual distance will vary with the type of pictures you're showing and the focal length of the lens in the projector.

Projector height: a minimum of 54 inches when people are seated in standard dining chairs.

MUSIC

Whether your children like to pound out a rock beat on a set of drums or you like to quietly play the piano while enjoying a cup of coffee, a place to make music encourages better harmony in the home. But don't jump right in, push aside furniture in the basement rec room, and begin to play. Plan carefully and choose a spot that will complement the sounds of the instruments and allow the entire family to gather as an audience.

All that's missing from the sunny room *at right* is a budding concert pianist. The room's design and furnishings—the tongue-and-groove white cedar wall, soft wall hanging, and area rug—all serve to enhance the music.

Good vibrations

Unless it's acoustically balanced, a music room will "color" the sound of live or recorded music. To determine the sonic character of the room you plan to use, stand in the center of the room, clap your hands, and speak in a loud voice. If you detect any ringing or echoing, your room is overly "bright" or "live," with too many hard surfaces reflecting sound waves. Adding carpet, rugs, draperies, or wall hangings will solve this problem.

If, on the other hand, the sharp sound of your clap seems lifeless and your voice sounds dull and muffled, the room is acoustically "dead" because soft surfaces are soaking up the sound waves. To make the room come alive, remove some of the heavily upholstered furnishings and thick rugs. If that's not possible, simply open the heavy draperies during performances to expose hard window glass. Or you can add a few glass-covered pictures to the walls.

When you're adding or taking away furnishings, try to strike a balance of hard and soft surfaces on opposite walls. For instance, if you hang heavy draperies on one wall, try to cover the opposite wall with hard-surfaced pictures.

Sound out the options

If you want to stop the music from drifting into the rest of the house, plan to make interior walls the soft surfaces and exterior walls the hard surfaces.

And, if there are rooms above the music room, consider a ceiling that absorbs sound and a floor with a hard surface. Acoustical ceiling tiles made of cellulose or mineral fiber work best. The tiles' pores trap tiny sound waves and absorb middle and high frequencies. The lower frequencies, which travel out in every direction, will still come through, but unless a person is playing the upright bass or tuba, the sound probably won't be bothersome.

If you do wish to block out lower frequencies, you can place sound-deadening board or foam panels directly above or to the side of the musician.

To use them most effectively, suspend acoustical tiles by a ceiling grid. A second, but less effective, option is to attach them to furring strips nailed to the ceiling. A sprayed acoustical plaster ceiling is an alternative to tiles, but it's the least effective method.

NUMBERS TO KNOW

Piano sizes:
- Grand, 58 to 60 inches wide by 70 to 81 inches deep (average Parlor Grand is 75 inches deep and weighs 700 pounds).
- Baby Grand, 53 to 58 inches wide by 49 to 68 inches deep.
- Upright, 57 to 60 inches wide by 23 to 26 inches deep, 36 to 48 inches high (average weight is 400 to 500 pounds).
- Electric Organs, 46 to 57 inches wide by 43 to 48 inches deep, 38 to 49 inches high (average weight is 220 to 550 pounds).

SMALL TABLE
GAMES

Small table games are great for getting the whole family together —or for a quiet twosome. They're inexpensive, don't take up much space, and usually appeal to people of all ages. If your family loves board games, choose a spot where everyone can sit comfortably. If you're an ace at bridge or poker, pick a place where the lighting is good and where you can easily set up a table. And if high-tech video games are your forte, make room to play around the television set.

A low table like the one shown *opposite* is perfect for board games because you can either sit on the floor or pull up chairs to play. In any case, when you're designing or shopping for tables, know how much space it takes to play your favorite games.

If you don't feel like hauling out a card table every time you want to play bridge or poker, consider a table with a split personality. The designer of the room pictured *below* planned the space for both frequent card games and casual dining. The two hinged tops covering the small table can be unfolded to transform the surface into a large Parsons table. The chairs are especially comfortable for extended evenings that start with supper and end with cards.

If you prefer backgammon or chess, you might choose a game table with a reversible top that features a game board on one or both sides.

Electronic wonders
In addition to the traditional board games, electronic games have hit Americans with a jolt. You may have seen them demonstrated in television commercials by enthusiastic people who clutch the games in their hands or laps. But to play them comfortably, both the master control boxes and small self-contained electronic games should be placed on a table. With video games, players have individual control boxes that they can either hold in their hands or place on a tabletop.

Home computers are one step up from video games. Most computers allow you to play video games, as well as store household information and other kinds of programs. If you plan to play games on your computer frequently, you may want to hook it to the television set, just as you would a video game. Otherwise, you'll probably need a separate television screen, or monitor, for

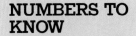

NUMBERS TO KNOW

Floor space required for a card table that seats four people: 48x48x30 inches high.

Recommended lighting plan for a game table that seats four people: four overhead reflector spotlights placed about two feet outside the corners of the game table.

the computer and a quiet place to put it where you can work or study alone.

Lighting for leisure activities
Adequate lighting is not only essential for the games described here, it's equally important for all the activities mentioned in this chapter.

To give you an idea of how much light you'll need for tabletop games and other activities, consider that one 75-watt light bulb provides 30 lumens of light on a surface three feet from the bulb, and direct sunlight provides 200 lumens inside a house a few feet from a window (a lumen is a standard for measuring light; you'll find lumen ratings on a bulb's paper sleeve, but not on the bulb itself). To play tabletop games, you need a minimum of 40 lumens. To read music scores (see page 106), you need 35 to 85 lumens. Lighting needs for other activities are listed on the following pages.

BIG TABLE GAMES

Table tennis and pool have long been favorite pastimes of families with ample space in their homes for fun and games. They're still popular, but people with more limited space have discovered other big table games and hobbies that take up less floor space. Instead of the traditional ball games, today's rec room is just as likely to have a pinball machine or a home exercise center. When you do find table tennis and pool, they sometimes appear in unfamiliar forms. Both games are now available in smaller sizes, and, unlike their predecessors, they fit in just about any room.

All these activities require ample floor space, so measure your room, and compare the results to the sizes of game tables and playing areas *before* you buy any equipment.

If you love to play pool but don't have much space, a bumper pool table is a good alternative. Space, however, is not a problem for the pool-playing family on the *opposite* page. Though the table is in a loft, there's enough room to allow tricky shots on all sides of the table.

If you're planning to purchase a pool table, don't think you can't furnish the area around it. You can easily move in low tables and seating as long as there is space for a player to stand and room over the furniture for free movement of the cue.

Like pool, table tennis requires room for the players to move. Make sure you have enough space for the table and playing area. Unlike pool, table tennis also requires rapid movement. For that reason, keep furnishings and low-hanging light fixtures out of the way so players don't stmble over them or hit them with a ball or paddle. Nonslip flooring is another necessity.

And if you like both table tennis *and* pool, consider this option: a table tennis top that will fit over your pool table.

There are, of course, other big hobbies for large rooms. Watching movies or slides, developing photos in a darkroom, and exercising indoors are all increasing in popularity because of new equipment that makes them more affordable and more adaptable to rooms of varying sizes.

NUMBERS TO KNOW

- Pool tables, typical sizes: 36x72 inches, 42x84 inches, 48x96 inches, and 54x108 inches. (Table weights range from 150 to 800 pounds.)
 Playing areas for small to large pool tables (with medium-length cue of 52 inches): 137x168 inches to 168x216 inches.
- Table tennis table, standard size: 60x108x30 inches; playing area: 156x276 inches.
- Other games, typical sizes: bumper pool, 53x38x30 inches; shuffleboard with side cushions, 22x112x32 inches; pinball, 26x62x68 inches; and air hockey, 84x42x30 inches.

- Lighting recommendations for pool table: one 40-watt fluorescent fixture, or two 150-watt, or three 100-watt silver bowl reflector fixtures hung low over the surface of the table and shaded on top and sides.
- Lighting recommendation for table tennis: ceiling floodlight over each end of the table.
- Typical screen sizes for movies and slides: 30x40 inches to 72x96 inches (tripod and wall or ceiling mounted roll-up screens).

CRAFTS/
SEWING

Sewing and crafts can be time-consuming if you're not organized. Because both hobbies require lots of tools and materials, storing them efficiently separates the good room—where everything's in place —from the bad room —where everything's misplaced. Keep items where you can put your hands on them quickly. Otherwise, you'll probably have to spread what you need temporarily on a table and spend precious time rummaging through boxes and clutter.

The best first step in setting up a sewing and crafts room is to make a list of the supplies you'll need and plan where to put them when they're not in use. Of course, a few items, such as a sewing machine and ironing board, should be at the top of your list. Decide where you'll put the basic tools, then look for spaces near the work area to put shallow drawers for tools and thread, deep drawers for fabrics, and cabinets or closets for storing the machine and other bulky items.

If building standard storage areas isn't feasible, think of something new. Picture, for example, a round cart with locking casters, drawers, and a wide surface area. With a few changes, you could put a sewing machine on top, store supplies inside, and wheel the cart into the nearest closet.

For a custom-built sewing and crafts center, select an out-of-the-way place so you can leave some of the clutter out on a table when you're not working on a project.

Look at the photos on these two pages. The hobbyist in this house squeezed a place to work from an unoccupied porch connecting two upstairs bedrooms. The area *opposite* includes a fold-down plastic laminate counter that serves as a cutting table and as a crafts center. The perforated

hardboard walls easily support open shelving.

The sewing counter *below* doubles as a planning desk. The nearby window provides welcome daylight.

If you're going to sew in the evenings, put some light on the subject. The track fixtures shown *opposite* are one example of how to do it right.

The nice extras

When planning your room, try to incorporate features that will make it even more functional:

• When you're choosing a table for a cutting surface, measure it first. It should hold a full length of unfolded fabric.
• Try mounting a full-length mirror on a nearby wall or closet door. If you have the space, put in a three-sided mirror.
• Use a padded stool or straight chair without arms at the sewing counter; you'll be able to move more freely.
• Set up the ironing board near an outlet where it won't get in the way.

NUMBERS TO KNOW

Minimum lighting requirements for sewing:
• Occasional periods, large stitches: 40 lumens.
• Occasional periods, light fabrics: 60 lumens.
• Prolonged periods, light to medium fabrics: 120 lumens.
• Prolonged periods, dark fabrics: 240 lumens.

Standard sizes for sewing cabinets:
26 to 37 inches wide x 20 to 30 inches deep x 30 inches high.

WET BARS

Just as our drinking tastes have changed (evident in the nation's shift to wine and lighter alcoholic spirits), so, too, have our tastes in home wet bars. No longer is the stand-up bar with padded-vinyl front edge the standard. Although still popular, it's not the only way to make the rounds. Adaptability is the key. If you entertain often and have the space for it, a traditional setup—with storage for glassware and bottles and possibly even a bar sink or refrigerator— could be best for you. On the other hand, if your tastes are simpler, you may just want to add a small wine rack to almost any spot on any shelf.

tors, heating pipes, and radiators. Ideally, the storage area should stay at 55 to 60 degrees Fahrenheit. If the temperature near the bar varies widely, consider storing your wine somewhere else, such as the basement or an attached garage.

If you do store wine elsewhere, you probably select only enough bottles for each occasion. If so, your bar could be part of a simple wall unit. The custom-built system, *left*, accommodates bottles, decanters, and accessories on only a couple of shelves.

If you're strapped for floor space, make the bar surface work doubly hard by using it as a buffet, and place bottles into a recessed area in a wall. The 7-foot built-in unit *below* has a bounty of closed storage as well as a striking wall display formed by the recessed bottles.

Finally, the light should be right in every bar. Choose subtle general lighting; accent lighting for displayed glassware and wine bottles; and soft task lighting for opening bottles, mixing drinks, etc.

For many people, wine bars or simple setups serve their needs nicely. For example, the rolling wine cart *opposite* will follow wherever you go. (It's topped with a no-stain serving surface.) But its real home is under a counter. The racks, originally built to hold shoes, keep a double row of wine bottles at the right angle so the cork stays moist and the sediment goes to the bottom where it belongs. And when you push the cart under a counter, harmful sunlight can't reach the bottles.

When shutting out the light, make sure the bottles don't feel the heat produced by ranges, dishwashers, refrigera-

NUMBERS TO KNOW

- Height of typical bar: 3 feet.
- Height of stand-up bar: 3 feet 6 inches.
- Minimum depth of bar: 12 inches.
- Minimum height of cabinet over bar or wine rack: 16 inches.
- Minimum shelf depth for glassware/bottle storage: 6 inches.
- Shelf space (6-inch shelf) required for one dozen glasses: pilsner, 24 inches; wine, 16 inches; champagne, 38 inches; beer, 32 inches; cocktail, 18 inches; old-fashioned, 24 inches.
- Dimension of accessories: bar sinks, 15 inches square to 15x25 inches; preferred faucets, 8- or 10-inch gooseneck; undercounter refrigerator, 18½ to 37⅝ inches wide and 18⅞ to 34⅜ inches high; ice maker, 15 to 17⅞ inches wide and 25¾ to 34½ inches high.

INDOOR GARDENING

Do you ever dream of putting a little bit of paradise into your home —a place where you can grow houseplants, flowers for cutting, even vegetables for the table? Well, dream no more; the age of the affordable greenhouse is here. No longer does it take thousands of dollars and an army of architects to make a greenhouse. A sunny window entranceway, patio, or neglected corner can become a lush oasis of living plants—cactus, primrose, palm, fern, geranium, begonia, and African violets will all thrive. In fact, if you have the proper lighting, you can grow almost anything.

Probably the quickest way to build a greenhouse is to install one in a sun-drenched window. Specially designed, glassed-in units are available from several manufacturers, but you can also build your own from readily available materials. For example, if an interior wall or entranceway gets abundant sunlight, convert it to a greenhouse wall by forming a lean-to with discarded storm windows placed against the wall. Or build a wood-frame lean-to to fit the space, and stretch heavy-duty plastic over the frame.

Light up your life
To create a hanging garden effect, add a skylight. The best plants to grow under skylights are trailing vines, available in both blossoming and foliage varieties. Keep in mind, however, that glass-enclosed gardens get plenty of sun but may become overheated on bright, sunny days, so provide adequate ventilation.

The green room
The prefabricated commercial greenhouse is the most desirable—and most expensive—option. But if you plan carefully, it will add solar heat to your home, and you may be able to recover the investment in a few years. The owners of the 8-foot-square commercial greenhouse *at right* chose it as a way to enlarge their cramped kitchen. Once the greenhouse was built, the family liked it so much that they installed track lighting so the room could be used in the evenings, too.

Good directions
Any greenhouse should be built in the direction that will offer the greatest amount of sun-light. Preferably, that direction is south, but you can also place it pointing southeast, southwest, or west. A northern exposure is suitable if you're growing only foliage plants. Wherever you place them, most plants need at least three hours of sunlight per day.

At the same time, check the indoor weather conditions before adding a greenhouse. Most homes are too warm, which means the moisture content of the air is low. As a result, many plants, especially those requiring cooler temperatures, may languish and die. Most homes are also a patchwork of cool nooks and warm crannies. To you, these spots may only be annoying, but to plants, they represent miniature climates—perfect for some, but slow death for others. To forecast how well your plants may grow, place thermometers and humidity gauges (hygrometers) wherever you plan a greenhouse, and then record the measurements over a period of time. Once you've established your greenhouse, add a sun trap, so plants will have optimum light, warmth, and humidity.

When your little bit of paradise is green and growing, you'll have unlimited opportunities to experiment with many different plants. Different kinds of gardening, however, require some homework (using artificial lights, for example, or hydroponic growing systems). Many systems need special attention—new wiring, different lighting, extended plumbing runs. If so, take these needs into consideration *before* building your greenhouse. (For more about indoor gardening, see pages 60-63.)

PLAY SPACES

Children need a sense of place, a homey, cheerful spot to call their own. For that reason, the rooms described here aren't purely for fun and games; they're also small territories your child can grow up in. A bedroom may be a good first choice for play space; your child will feel that the room is a private retreat and not a place to share with grown-ups. (Of course, personal turf may also be the toughest for your child to keep clean.) The bedroom may offer the best play area, but don't rule out other areas of the house; if you have the space, by all means use it. But wherever you plan play space, make sure it's flexibly designed, a spot your child can grow into—comfortably.

For the most flexible room, you may want to design your own furnishings. The four-year-old *opposite* has plenty of space to store his toys in the modular corner cube (located between the two single-bed modulars). The beauty of the system is that it allows you to rearrange the 30-inch-high modulars and use them as a sofa-bed combination for an older child. So that the L-shaped unit doesn't move when the child is playing, each bed is bolted to the corner cube with easy-to-remove hardware. The gold wall, covered in burlap, is a handy place to tack up posters and pictures.

If you don't want to design and build furnishings for play space, try adapting regular household furnishings for pint-size needs. In the six-year-old's room *above*, a child can easily reach toys stored on two white modular shelves. Single-shelf units serve as play tables with matching chairs.

The bed is a twin-size mattress placed on cylindrical plastic storage units. A matching storage cart on wheels can accommodate the odds and ends of almost any hobby

(in this case, finger paints). Track-mounted light fixtures have retractable cords, so a child can pull the lights down when playing on the floor or working at the desk, then raise the lights after they're finished.

To convert this room into a teenager's retreat, just stack the shelves higher and continue to use the plastic units for storage.

Safety tips

A play space must be a safe place. Remember these do's and don'ts when you're designing a play area:

• Don't use toy chests or vertical storage cabinets with hinged lids or doors that swing upward. Falling lids have caused numerous deaths and head injuries in recent years.

• Whenever possible, use storage chests or cabinets without lids or doors. If you do buy cabinets with doors, make sure they have piano hinges that allow them to open fully.

• Likewise, make sure all hardware has rounded edges and is unbreakable. Try to avoid buying or building children's furniture with sharp corners and angles.

• Don't use small area rugs on wood or resilient flooring without tacking them to the floor. Children can easily slip on small rugs.

• Make sure lighting fixtures are well protected from flying objects and young children who might try to unscrew light bulbs.

• If you're using open storage, place the lighter objects on the top shelves.

NUMBERS TO KNOW

Lighting recommendations for play spaces of different sizes: small, under 150 square feet; average, 185 to 250 square feet; and large, over 250 square feet.

Wattage for suspended or surface-mounted incandescent fixtures: small, one fixture with three to five bulbs totaling 150 to 200 watts; average, two or more fixtures with four to six bulbs totaling 200 to 300 watts; and large, one fixture per 125 square feet and one watt per square foot.

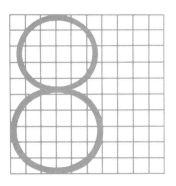

KEEPING WARM WITH WOOD

A young American inventor named Benjamin Franklin once solved a colonial energy crisis. At the time, fireplaces were woefully inefficient, gobbling huge amounts of air and wood, then sending most of the precious heat straight up undampered chimneys. So much wood was being consumed that supplies of firewood began to disappear. To solve the problem, Franklin set about inventing his famous stove. It worked then—and works now. But even old Ben would be impressed by some of the thoroughly modern wood heaters described in this chapter.

CHOOSING A WOOD ENERGY UNIT

If you're thinking about putting wood's energy to work at your house, you're not alone. Millions of American homes are now partially or totally heated with wood stoves, fireplaces, or furnaces—and more families are turning to wood every year.

So chances are, you're already familiar with the way modern wood-heating units function. By throttling airflow so the fire gets no more oxygen than it really needs, the stoves burn not just the wood itself, but also combustible gases that the sizzling logs give off. The result: a fire that burns hotter and lasts longer without tending than even the frugal Dr. Franklin might have envisioned.

But before you rush out to buy the latest, fanciest wood-burning stove, consider the commitment you must make to burning wood as a source of heat. Henry Thoreau, a passionate naturalist, hit on part of the problem when he wrote, "Wood heats you twice, once when you cut it, and again when you burn it."

He could have added that you can also stay warm carrying the stuff inside, cleaning up bark chips and other debris that form a temporary trail wherever you go, taking out messy ashes, cleaning the flue, maintaining the chimney, and a score of extra chores needed to keep a wood burner in safe operating condition. You'll need, in short, a steely dedication to burning wood for heat.

At the same time, much has been made about the ecological impact of heating with wood. No one has all the answers yet, but some things are obvious. For example, wood smoke sometimes stinks. Just being downwind from a nearby campfire can be an annoying,

choking experience. In addition, restrictive fire codes and the burdensome tasks of transporting and storing large supplies of wood could make heating the old-fashioned way too impractical for folks in big cities and densely populated suburbs.

On the other hand, it's obvious that out in the open, wood smoke isn't especially harmful. Unlike coal and oil, it doesn't dump sulfur on our surroundings. In fact, it leaves behind nothing that normal oxidation from decay doesn't deposit more slowly.

If everyone falls in love with wood, however, what will happen to all the lovely trees? Some people think our forests may disappear if millions of would-be Paul Bunyans start taking an ax to them. That's not really true. Even the American Forest Institute, which needs trees to stay in business, notes that lumber required for building will grow quicker, stronger, and straighter if forests are culled of slow-growing hardwoods and less useful varieties. So, even in the eyes of the timber industry, a solid wood market is desirable.

One increasingly common place to put our wealth of wood is a fireplace insert like the one pictured *opposite* and on the following page. Inserts, which more or less slide into an existing masonry fireplace, are heating up the public's fancy because they're easy to install and they put out comfortably even warmth over a relatively long period of time. The insert *opposite* provides up to 12 hours of heat on a single fueling of wood. Although designed primarily to burn wood, this model can be converted to handle coal just by substituting a special grate.

(continued)

CHOOSING A WOOD-ENERGY UNIT
(continued)

The wood-burning unit for you depends on many things—your needs, your tastes, and your budget. One of the four units illustrated on these two pages may offer just what you're looking for.

Ordinary fireplaces and most stoves blast heat into a room via radiation; the closer to the fire you are, the warmer you will be. Unfortunately, much of the warmth goes up the chimney. An old-fashioned fireplace may suck out some of your furnace-heated air, too. With a modern insert in your fireplace, however, you can solve those problems. Study the drawing *at upper right* and you can see how an insert pulls in room air, wraps it around the firebox, then sends it out in natural convection currents (sometimes enhanced by a small fan or blower).

As with any good wood-burning unit, an insert cuts down on trips to the woodpile and the amount of ashes you need to haul out. Unlike the stoves described later, most inserts have doors you can open to enjoy the aura of a conventional fireplace.

Opening the doors, of course, negates the unit's airtightness—its draft will be uncontrolled and much less efficient. But open fires build up much less creosote in the flue (see the safety tips on page 125), so some wood-heat families like to open up the doors during the day when they need less heat, then bank the fire and close the doors at bedtime.

Heat-circulating fireplaces

Are you thinking about a fireplace for your new or present home? Invest only in an air-circulator unit—ideally one with glass doors and outside air intakes like the prefab version illustrated *at lower right*.

These are relatively efficient house-heaters, capable of backing up a passive or active solar heating system or letting a conventional furnace relax for long periods of time.

Part of their efficiency is due to the heat-proof glass doors. They help to regulate the draft, just as the iron doors do on a fireplace insert or an airtight stove. But the doors on a prefab let you enjoy the flames.

Don't let the term *prefab* throw you, either. There's nothing chintzy (or inexpensive) about a heat-circulating fireplace. Some units, like this one, require the same costly footings and masonry work as an ordinary fireplace—*plus* a welded-steel, double-shell firebox and ducting to the various rooms you want to heat.

Masonry-and-steel units last a lifetime, but you can save quite a bit of money by dispensing with the brick or stone work entirely and simply framing in a zero-clearance model.

Zero-clearance fireplaces put a heat-circulator's cool outer shell to good use. Efficient wood-burners put out temperatures of 1,000 degrees or more, enough to dry out and set afire any combustibles, such as wood, wallpaper, and paneling, that are within a foot or so of the unit. Circulating a thick blanket of air around a hot inner liner not only warms air in the room, but it also cuts to zero the chance that the unit's shell will ignite adjacent framing, walls, or floors.

Installing a zero-clearance, heat-circulating fireplace is a relatively simple carpentry job. Face it with brick or stone, and no one has to know you didn't lay up the entire project with trowel and mortar.

Check local fire codes before you invest in a zero-clearance unit. Not all models meet all community requirements.

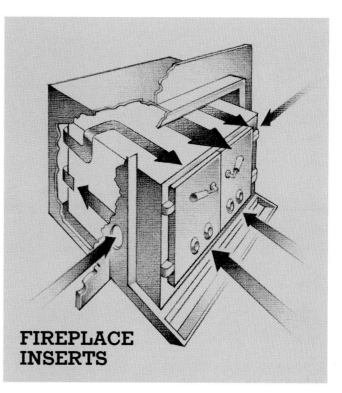

FIREPLACE INSERTS

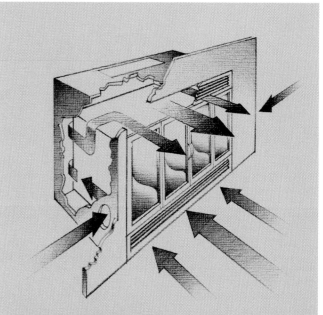

HEAT-CIRCULATING FIREPLACE

Airtights

If you've heard the claims for today's new generation of wood stoves, you understandably may be skeptical. Can these units really burn all night on a single load of logs, leave so few ashes that you need to clean them out only once a week, and extract just about every BTU of heat that wood has to offer? (Heat from any source is rated in British thermal units, or BTUs.)

The answers are yes, yes, and yes—if the model is a true airtight. Because you can regulate the draft through them, airtights let you fine-tune a fire to reach its most efficient level of heat.

Airtights are available in numerous models. Almost all of them distill the wood with a variation of the baffle arrangements shown in the illustration *at upper right*. Air enters only at an adjustable intake and flows through in an S-pattern that holds heat within the stove.

Airtights fall into three general categories—cast-iron, steel, and heat circulating. We'll discuss the pros and cons of these basic types of airtights on pages 128 and 129.

Multifuel furnace units

All of the multifuel furnace units on the market have one feature in common—they can supply heat by burning wood alone, or they can be used along with almost any other central heating unit, including a heat pump.

How is it possible? Remember that a furnace is nothing more than a centrally located source of heat, with a system for distributing the warmth it creates to other parts of the house. Whether heat is created by oil, gas, electricity, coal, or wood is irrelevant—except that

wood may provide the cheapest source of energy.

In a wood-burning furnace, fuel is burned in an airtight firebox. Sophisticated draft controls limit the amount of air that enters the combustion chamber, so heat output is maintained at a steady level. In fact, most of the better units have a thermostat to keep the temperatures uniform. Air heated around the combustion chamber is fed into a plenum for distribution through ducts. Other self-contained units have a boiler—again heated by oil, gas, or wood—that distributes hot water to radiators or baseboard units.

Some units are totally self-contained—the unit will burn wood, oil, or gas. But you don't have to start from scratch to have central wood heat, either. More than a dozen manufacturers offer units intended for installation next to your existing furnace.

The diagram *at lower right* shows how one of the units works. Cold air traveling from the air-return registers in your house enters the back of the unit where it's warmed by the firebox. The heated air then exits through a duct leading to the existing furnace for distribution through the hot-air ductwork. The blower in your regular furnace provides the air pressure to distribute the warmth to all parts of your house.

Before investing in a multifuel unit, you have to be committed to burning wood as a source of heat. For one thing, a wood furnace will cost more than a wood stove, and the labor required to install it is significant. Unlike the smaller, freestanding units, you can't simply sell it if you lose your enthusiasm for wood heat—it's part of your house.

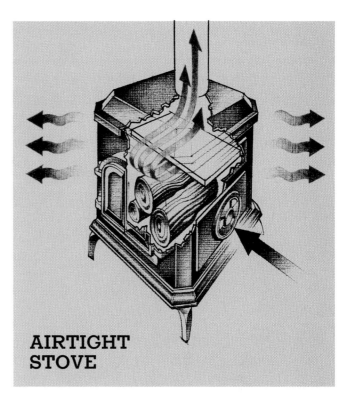

AIRTIGHT STOVE

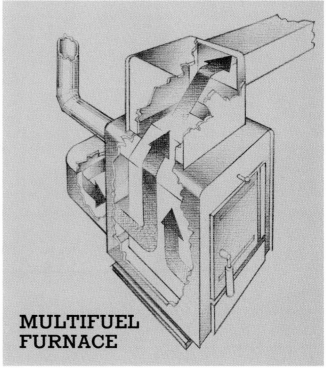

MULTIFUEL FURNACE

MAKING AN EXISTING FIREPLACE MORE EFFICIENT

If your home is equipped with one of the nation's 20 million masonry fireplaces, you've probably enjoyed many cozy evenings watching its crackling fires. But what you *couldn't* watch was the endless trail of heated air escaping up the chimney. What you wouldn't have *enjoyed* was the knowledge that your fireplace may actually be eating more air—valuable warm household air—than it's heating, leaving your furnace to make up the deficit.

But don't board up your fireplace yet! There are much better ways to solve the problem.

One simple solution is to install glass doors. They'll help to prevent a fire from consuming the air in your home and, at the very least, they'll provide a way to seal off the fireplace when you go to bed—before the fire goes out and you can close the damper.

Warm up to an insert

Installing an insert like those pictured *at left* can improve the efficiency of your fireplace 40 to 60 percent and turn it into a comfortable source of heat.

Dozens of firms manufacture numerous fireplace inserts, most of which will fit into your fireplace opening. But before you begin comparing models, first check the territory. Inspect your chimney carefully (see the box *opposite* and the additional safety tips on page 131). Now, take a look at the hearth extension (the noncombustible flat area directly in front of the fireplace opening) and the flooring nearby. Take some measurements, then decide how far the insert can project into the room and if you'll need to protect the floor with a stove mat. (Also, be sure to check local codes.)

Your next move is to the mantel and other flammable objects close to the fireplace. Note how far they are from the fireplace opening.

Finally, check your bank account. You will need $700 to $1,000 for the insert and accessories and $400 to $700 for a flue lining, if necessary.

As you weigh the merits of various inserts, keep these guidelines in mind:
• *Size*. Ideally, you simply slide the insert's self-contained firebox into your old masonry firebox, seal off the rest of the old opening with a surround plate, and start a fire. (Some manufacturers suggest that you remove the old damper, while others say you can simply secure it in the open position.)

The amount of metal *outside* the firebox varies from brand to brand. In fact, some units are more "outserts" than inserts, so be sure to measure carefully before you shop. The insert shown *at lower left* is really an outsert because it stands on the hearth, outside the firebox of a masonry fireplace; only a duct extends into the old cavity.
• *Baffles*. Most fireplace inserts have metal baffles that lead the products of combustion to the exit. As hot gases flow past the baffles, the metal surfaces absorb a substantial number of BTUs before they can escape through the chimney. This process heats the insert to the point where it draws in room air at the bottom, heats the air, and expels it back into the room at the top.
• *Shell configuration*. If the unit has a single shell (just one layer of metal), the insert warms the room by radiating heat through its shell. Most inserts, however, have double or triple walls throughout; all things being equal, these models will deliver the most heat.
• *Materials*. Most fireplace inserts are made from cast iron

or heavy-gauge steel, and both materials work fine. A few manufacturers, however, use light alloys such as galvanized steel, aluminized steel, and stainless steel.

• *Weight*. Inserts made from heavy metal and/or lined with firebrick are slow to warm up but they store more heat, put out more even heat, and cool off more slowly than lighter models do.

• *Vent exits*. The exit for combustion gases may be in the rear, on top, or in a sloped area between the rear and top. You may, in fact, find one, two, or more openings— round, square, or rectangular. The design of the exit is especially important, because the openings should be located where they'll provide the most direct, unobstructed path to your existing damper. More and more builders are recommending that you install a flue connector between the unit's exit point and your damper.

• *Blower*. This device gives a mechanical boost to the natural convective airflow.

• *Screen*. Screens are usually available as an option; buying one is worth the investment if you use the insert with the doors open.

• *Grates*. A wood grate has a unique shape, so be sure you get the right one for your insert. Check to see if the grate has andirons or another feature to stop logs from rolling forward into the doors.

• *Interlock*. When an insert's adjustable damper isn't fully open, the fire can flash out if you open the doors suddenly. To prevent this, some manufacturers equip their inserts with a system that locks the doors when the damper is closed.

Fixing a faulty draw
If your fireplace won't give up

smoking, there are a number of ways to break the habit.

First, make sure it's getting an adequate supply of oxygen —not too much, not too little. Open the damper, wet a finger, and stick it into the firebox. If you feel air rushing from above, there's a downdraft strong enough to smoke up your house or kill the fire.

To augment the amount of inside air available to the fire, shut off all exhaust fans in the house. Also, open a window near the fireplace.

If these methods fail, consider one or more of the following solutions: check the damper to make sure it's fully open; clean soot or mortar off the smoke shelf; clean out the vent brick, or, if none exists, think about installing one; add firebricks at the back or sides of the fireplace; use a grate to raise the fire; or install a chimney fan.

Check your roof, too. For a good draw, a chimney must be at least two feet higher than any nearby buildings or trees. New construction in the area may be causing your problem.

Checking for flue problems
The chimney on your roof may have several different flues —one for each fireplace, plus additional vents for the furnace and water heater.

A defective flue is potentially dangerous. Obviously, it may set the house on fire, but, less obviously, a leaky flue or a strong downdraft could also pull poisonous carbon monoxide into your home.

To ward off both of these hazards, modern chimneys have firebrick linings or flue tiles that rarely leak. If you own an older home, don't use a fireplace that's been out of action until a professional has checked the flue. He may recommend a metal liner like the one illustrated *at right*.

(For more on this important subject, see pages 130 and 131.)

DO YOU HAVE A SAFE CHIMNEY?

If you're adding a fireplace insert, be sure to have a professional mason check out your existing chimney and flue; they may be damaged. Also, it's extremely important to check the inside of the chimney and flue lining (if you have one) for a coating of dark goop called *creosote*. If you find more than a quarter-inch layer, have a chimney sweep remove it. Heavy creosote deposits, when ignited, can quickly become a full-blown chimney blaze —and possibly a fire that could destroy your whole house. (For more on this important subject, see pages 130 and 131.)

Climb onto the roof and look at the mortar joints. If you see a dark, oily seepage—again, creosote— have the joints repaired.

Once the chimney and flue lining are clean and in good repair, don't forget about them entirely—be sure to have the chimney passage cleaned at least once a year.

Lining up the odds
A new, correctly sized flue lining can increase the efficiency of your insert *and* improve the safety of your chimney. One of the products on the market—a factory-built stainless steel flue lining, illustrated *at upper right*—has at least four advantages.

• It reduces the buildup of creosote by maintaining a much higher temperature on the surface of the flue lining. Unburned volatile substances aren't as likely

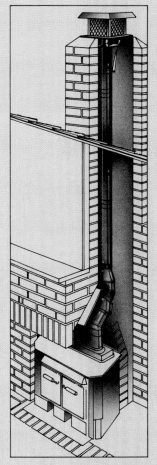

to condense as creosote on such a hot surface.

• The lining buffers a masonry chimney against large temperature swings, thereby reducing cracks that result from normal expansion and contraction.

• It provides excellent updraft, because the compact lining (smaller than the original flue tiles) increases the velocity of the draft.

• Finally, and perhaps most important, the flue lining comes in a kit that's simple to install.

RESTYLING
A FIREPLACE

No matter how heated your love is for the fireplace you have now, there may come a time when you will want to restyle it. And that's only natural. A fireplace often dominates the overall look and feeling of a room.

In the restyling shown *opposite*, the homeowners achieved a nice balance between heavy mass and exquisite detail by fashioning a brand-new mantel from railroad ties and delicate Dutch tiles. The two dissimilar materials complement each other and contribute a pleasant blend of country styles to the overall look of the room.

You can also replace your mantel by ordering an antique wood or marble version, or even a new wood one.

Dismantling a mantel

Before you can install a new mantel, however, you'll probably have to remove the old one. You can do this in a variety of ways, depending on how the old mantel was installed. With well-crafted styles, finishing nails and screws may almost defy detection. So, take a close look to figure out the kinds of fasteners used and where they're located.

Wood parts joined by nails can usually be tapped apart with a hammer and a block of wood. To get at screws, you may have to drill or scrape away a concealing plug of wood or filler.

If you're thinking about reusing any of the parts, dismantling a mantel can be an especially painstaking job. If you're not, all you need to be careful of are the structural elements you're going to attach the new mantel to.

Installing a mantel

To install a new mass-produced or custom-made mantel, you usually have to first put up

furring strips. One furring strip should run horizontally above the firebox; two others should run vertically down either side.

Often, you'll find the back of the mantel recessed to fit over an arrangement of furring strips like this. If so, examine the back of the new mantel, take some measurements, and place the furring strips accordingly. Use a level to make sure everything is plumb.

After you've positioned the furring strips, the mantel should fit snugly right over them, as shown in the illustration *at upper right*. Attach it with nails or screws. Finishing nails usually will do the job.

Putting up a mantelpiece

A mantelpiece is the shelf itself. You can install one in a number of ways. Here are two separate methods.

If you're attaching a rough wood mantelpiece to a brick fireplace, as shown in the illustration *at middle right*, begin by cutting 5/8-inch steel rods to extend approximately 3½ inches into the brick and 50 percent of the fore-and-aft width of the mantelpiece. If the piece is 10 inches, for example, the rod will be 8½ inches long (5 inches plus 3½ inches).

Drill holes into the mantelpiece, and epoxy the rods into position. Then drill holes into the brick joint at the same spacing. Grout the attached rods into place, making sure the front is supported while the grout sets. (Epoxy grout works best.)

To attach a mantelpiece supported by corbels, as shown in the illustration *at lower right*, first install roundheaded screws above the fireplace. Make sure they're level and spaced to match the corbel brackets. They should protrude just enough to allow you to slide the corbels into position.

INSTALLING A STOCK MANTEL

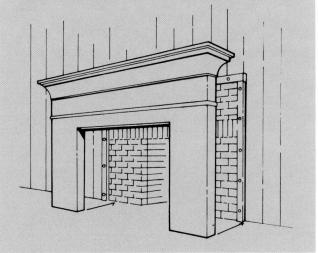

INSTALLING A MANTELPIECE

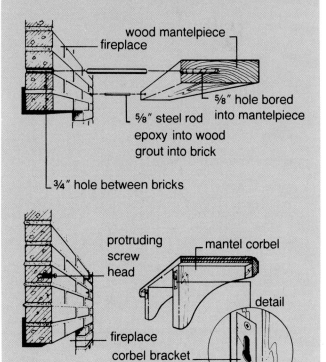

wood mantelpiece
fireplace
5/8" hole bored into mantelpiece
5/8" steel rod
epoxy into wood
grout into brick
3/4" hole between bricks

protruding screw head
mantel corbel
detail
fireplace
corbel bracket

SELECTING A WOOD-BURNING STOVE

A wood-burning stove will hold a warm spot in your house if you select and install it correctly.

Before choosing the kind you want, decide where to put the stove and the hearth it will rest on. The best location will have three distinct advantages.
• First, it will allow as much of the area as possible to be heated by the stove's radiant energy. (Placed near a stairway, for example, a stove can easily circulate warm air to upstairs rooms.)
• Second, it will be conveniently close to your stack of logs but will still permit you to maneuver easily around the stove as you're putting logs in or taking ashes out.
• Finally, and most important, it will be a safe spot, one that is reasonably inaccessible to small children and adequately clear from any combustible surfaces.

After finding the perfect spot for your wood stove, visit as many dealers as possible. Ask questions about materials, construction methods, accessories, options, and service. Just how "airtight" is the stove? Can the dealer install the unit immediately, or must you wait? How long is the guarantee and how inclusive?

Cast-iron basics

The most prized of all wood-heating units, cast-iron stoves are cozy ways to warm your home. Iron heats slowly and evenly. It cools gradually, too, which means warmth continues to radiate for hours after the last coals have died. Iron is legendarily durable, as well. And because iron can assume any shape in its molten state, makers of iron stoves are able to offer everything from exact replicas of elaborately ornate Victorian models to sleek, contemporary designs.

128

Cast-iron stoves are molded in parts, which are then machined and bolted together. All seams should snugly overlap to keep sparks in and unwanted air out. To make them even tighter, the seams may be caulked with furnace cement.

Occasionally, iron stoves can have drawbacks. Sudden temperature changes and sharp blows can fracture the brittle metal. And, when iron has been cracked, it's almost impossible to repair. To stave off the problem, season a new iron stove with small fires.

Stoves of steel

Steel stoves generally cost less than iron units. They heat up faster but also cool more quickly, although some units are lined with firebrick to help retain heat. The heavier the steel's gauge, the longer the unit will last—but eventually even the best will rust out.

When shopping for a steel stove, consider not only how thick the walls are, but also how well the door fits. The best units have cast-iron doors set into cast-iron frames and sealed with asbestos gaskets. Look, too, for baffles that can be taken out and flipped over when warping causes sags.

Heat-circulating stoves

The ultimate in fill-it-and-forget-it convenience, heat-circulating stoves feature double-wall construction that circulates air around the firebox to warm a room by convection as well as direct radiation. Some heat-circulating stoves also have blowers to help move the air and thermostat-regulated draft controls that will tend the fire automatically.

The main problem with heat-circulating units is that most of them have a dreary, furnace-like appearance that may not fit in with your room's decor.

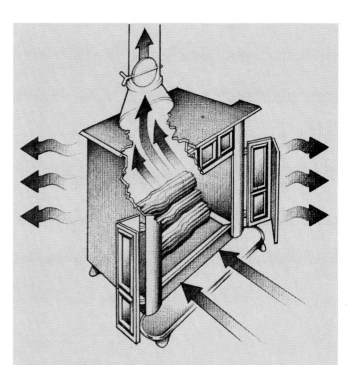

CHOOSING A FREE-STANDING FIREPLACE

Airtight stoves can warm your house, but they may not warm your heart. Because you can't see the flames, your romance with heating with wood may flicker and die.

Freestanding fireplaces offer a good compromise. Opening the door(s) on units like the Franklin, *above*, or Scandinavian-made combination unit, *opposite*, sacrifices efficiency but adds atmosphere. When you close them, both are excellent heaters, especially the combination unit.

All freestanding fireplaces have the advantage of an exposed chimney pipe, which radiates additional warmth. And because the whole unit is exposed, you don't waste precious time and money framing it in.

Most freestanding fireplaces can go almost anywhere, but check local building codes before installing your unit. Once the unit is in place on a fireproof base, you simply run interlocking lengths of chimney pipe through the ceiling to the roof.

Hearth requirements vary, but most need a noncombustible base that extends 18 inches from the front and sides of the fireplace and a minimum of 36 inches from the back. A thin concrete slab, bricks or tiles mortared together, or a wood frame filled with loose gravel will work well. Some well-insulated freestanding units don't require a noncombustible hearth; they have legs that can rest directly on a wood floor.

LIVING WITH A WOOD-HEAT UNIT

THE ECONOMICS OF WOOD HEAT

The economics of heating with wood are difficult to determine. First you have to consider the original price of the unit, along with any installation charges. If wood is your only source of heat, these costs would naturally replace those you'd incur installing gas, oil, or electric heating. If wood is a supplementary source of heat, then you have to determine how much it allows you to cut down on using your other heating systems—assuming, obviously, that burning wood for warmth is less expensive than the other sources of heat.

The price of wood itself varies widely—all the way from practically free to as much as $200 per cord. The chart *below* can give you some idea how the cost of wood measures up against the cost of oil.

The figures across the bottom of the chart depict the cost of a gallon of No. 2 heating oil. The numbers at left represent the price of a cord of split, air-dried hardwood. The diagonal line represents the points at which the value per dollar's worth of cord wood equals that of fuel oil, or the break-even point for comparing costs of the two fuels.

If fuel oil doesn't get your furnace going, keep the following facts in mind as handy comparisons. One cord of wood contains *approximately* the same amount of potential energy as these fuels: electricity, 5,300 kilowatt-hours; oil, 200 gallons; coal, 1.1 tons; and gas, 24,160 cubic feet.

Cost of cord of wood

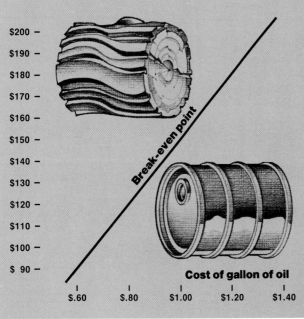

Break-even point

Cost of gallon of oil

$200 –
$190 –
$180 –
$170 –
$160 –
$150 –
$140 –
$130 –
$120 –
$110 –
$100 –
$ 90 –

$.60 $.80 $1.00 $1.20 $1.40

HOW TO SELECT FIREWOOD

Some kinds of wood are better than others. Hardwoods make the best fires. Because of their greater density, they burn more slowly and evenly than softwoods, while generating nearly twice the BTUs. An air-dried cord of hickory, for example, contains more than 30 million BTUs; an equivalent amount of ash, white pine, or basswood contains only 17 million. Other good woods with relatively high BTU ratings are red oak, yellow birch, soft maple, and tamarack.

The moisture content of the wood is also important. The higher it is, the less efficiently wood burns. Green or unaged wood, for example, not only contains much water, but it also contributes to the buildup of the potentially dangerous oil known as creosote.

If you do buy green wood—and sometimes you can save money by doing so—allow it to dry out. Store it for at least a year. And if you're keeping the wood outside, cover it with a loose-fitting plastic sheet.

Most dealers sell firewood by the *cord* (a stack of logs measuring eight feet long, four feet high, and four feet wide). However, not every dealer defines a cord in the same way. Some may quote prices on *face cords*, which are eight feet long and four feet high, but may be only one or two feet wide, depending on how long the logs were cut. A face cord of two-foot logs is, actually, only half a cord.

Other problems occur when buying wood by the truckful. Pickup trucks come in many different sizes, and interpretations of what makes up a "load" may vary greatly. Generally, however, you can estimate that one load will equal approximately one-third to one-half a cord.

Although it's convenient to have a dealer deliver and stack wood, you can save money—and burn up calories at the same time—by collecting firewood yourself. Stop at hardwood sawmills; they sometimes sell waste wood at low rates. Also check construction sites; you may be able to haul away felled trees if you obtain permission from the construction supervisor. Visit the sites of municipal projects; they may yield a harvest of wood as well. In addition, call the state and national conservation offices to find out if they issue permits for cutting trees in public forests.

Farmers who manage woodlots are one more source of inexpensive wood. When they thin out their lots, they may allow you to remove some trees. In the same way, homeowners may welcome you after a storm has downed trees on their property.

One final reminder: Even free wood has a price. In addition to paying for the cost of driving to and from the site, you may have to buy or rent a chain saw and splitting equipment to make the wood useable.

FIRE SAFETY FIRST AND ALWAYS

You needn't fear burning wood as a source of heat, but you must treat fire with respect. Consider these points carefully:

• *Clearances*. Keep your wood-burning unit a safe distance from any combustible surfaces. The National Fire Protection Agency (NFPA) recommends that all single-wall radiant heating units and stovepipes be a minimum of 36 inches from any combustible material or surface. Don't assume that brick or ceramic tile covering a combustible surface will provide adequate protection under 36 inches. It won't.

If you *do* put the unit closer than 36 inches from a combustible surface, be sure to shield the surface with a piece of sheet metal or mineral board. Leave at least one inch of space between the combustible surface and shield. For spacers, use ceramic insulators or metal wall studs commonly used in commercial construction. You can cover the combustible surface with any noncombustible decorative facing or fireproof paint and rest assured that the wall behind is safe.

Some units are tested in a laboratory and can be installed closer than 36 inches from combustible surfaces. If so, clearances should be clearly spelled out in the literature accompanying the unit.

• *Chimneys*. Checking the chimney should be at the top of your list. If you're planning to attach a wood-burning unit to an existing masonry chimney, ask a professional to inspect the chimney first. If it's more decorative than functional, the chimney is not likely to be safe to use with a wood-burning heater. Nor would a simple stovepipe on the outside of the house be safe to use.

The best chimneys are prefabricated metal units. Use the three-walled variety, with air spaces between layers of sheet metal, when you're installing a prefabricated fireplace. For airtight wood-burning units, use a two-layered chimney consisting of inner and outer walls with mineral wool insulation sandwiched between.

A clean, properly functioning chimney is so important because it cuts down on the buildup of a dirty and dangerous material known as creosote.

Your fire doesn't consume all the volatile substances produced by combustion. Some of these substances exit with the smoke but condense into a liquid form when the temperature drops to a certain level. After a time, this liquid hardens into a semi-solid mass (creosote) lining the chimney. When creosote builds to a thick layer, it's easily ignited by a hotter than normal fire in the stove or fireplace. Flames and sparks will start shooting out of your chimney, accompanied by a tremendous roar. The stovepipe will tremble and vibrate and may begin to glow red-hot. Flames may even begin to become visible through joints and seams in the stovepipe.

Obviously, then, it's important to reduce the buildup of creosote as much as possible. A cold chimney, such as a single-walled stovepipe on the outside of the house, contributes to the accumulation of creosote. The same is true of triple-wall chimneys intended for prefabricated fireplaces. (These chimneys, however, are safe for fireplaces, because a hearth fire generally is hotter than a stove fire, and most of the volatiles that condense into creosote are consumed.)

Even a sound masonry chimney isn't ideal. Its total mass allows for quick cooling before the smoke exits. And, because the inner flue generally is oversized for the stove, the smoke lingers on its way up, allowing even more condensation to take place.

The mineral-wool-packed units work well because they are hot chimneys. The same insulation that keeps the outer walls safely cool allows the inner surfaces to stay hot, minimizing condensation and the subsequent buildup of creosote.

• *Emergency action*. Fire! If you have an airtight unit, close all drafts and dampers to deprive the fire of air. If the fire is in a chimney attached to a fireplace, box heater, or Franklin stove, evacuate the house and call the fire department.

Like other potential hazards, all chimney fires are avoidable—just keep the chimney clean. Whenever creosote builds to a thickness approaching ¼ inch, the chimney should be thoroughly cleaned.

HOW TO BUILD A PERFECT FIRE

1. Open up the damper all the way. If you're not sure that it's open, look upward into the firebox. Use a flashlight, if necessary.

2. Crumple a few pieces of newspaper and put them on the floor of the firebox. Then arrange thin scraps of dry kindling (softwood works best) over the newspaper in a tepee formation.

3. Make sure at least some of the logs are split (none should be more than five inches in diameter). Put the largest one in first, at the back of the fireplace on the andirons or grate. Put a smaller log toward the front of the fireplace.

4. Place two split logs atop and parallel to the base logs. Leave some space between the logs so air can circulate around the fire.

5. Place another piece of newspaper on top of the logs and light it. Now light the kindling. Your fire should leap into life. (If it doesn't, your house may be sealed too tightly, the chimney obstructed, or a downdraft too strong.)

6. Replenish logs as they're consumed. To maintain a cheery blaze, you need at least three in the firebox. Periodically, prod and roll the logs over with a poker.

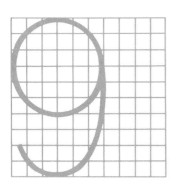

FAMILY CENTER PROJECTS YOU CAN BUILD

Buying furniture will test the limits of any budget. If you're looking for something to fit into one of your family centers—but every price tag you see brings a lump to your throat—why not build it yourself? This chapter describes how to make a wonderfully diverse set of projects—tables of all kinds, storage units, desks, and more. Before beginning, however, take a look at Chapters 5 and 6 to review the process of planning and building units like these.

TABLES

Handsome and practical, this oak coffee table measures 25½x32x16 inches. To build the top, cut two strips (A) of 1x3 flooring, with tongues-and-grooves removed. Butt together pieces of 1x3 flooring (B) to form the top. Glue and nail 1x3 spacers (C,D) to form the support assembly. Clamp the strips, spacers, and top together until the glue dries.

Cut a 45-degree edge along each end of the tabletop. Construct the sides (E,F,G,H) using the same procedure. Miter one end of each side panel. Join the sides to the top. Spread glue on all mitered surfaces; press top to sides with lumber to keep joints square.

Drill pilot holes, and nail the joints together, insetting the nails as you work. Fill the holes, then face the top's and the sides' outside edges with mitered oak strips (I,J). Add molding (K,L,M); sand, stain, and varnish the table.

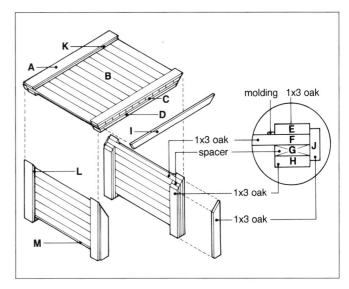

To make this 60x31¾-inch trestle table, first build the frame for the tabletop. Miter 1x4s, cut a 2x2 nailer to span the table's width, apply an even coat of glue to all ends, and clamp them together, making sure the frame is square. Drive two nails into each joint.

While waiting for the glue to dry, cut 1x4 planks for the top. Set them aside. (You can also build the top with flooring, using wide, tongue-and-groove pine or fir planks.)

Next, cut 2x4 legs (A,B) and 5/4x6 uprights (C) to size. Join each upright to the top and bottom 2x4, using two ½-inch dowels per joint. Glue, clamp, and let them dry.

Then cut 5/4x6 stretchers (D) to size. Notch the center of each to make room for the 2x2 nailer.

Now you are ready to assemble the pieces. Glue and screw the stretchers into place between the table legs. Nail and glue the leg assembly to the original tabletop frame, butting it against the inside and allowing a recess for the top planks.

Nail on the top planks, spacing them a fraction of an inch apart. Fill the nail holes. Sand, stain, and varnish the table, or seal it with polyurethane.

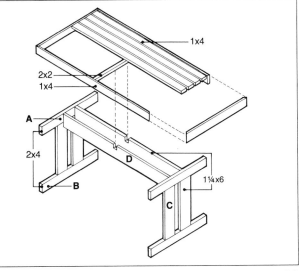

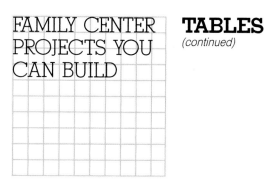
TABLES

(continued)

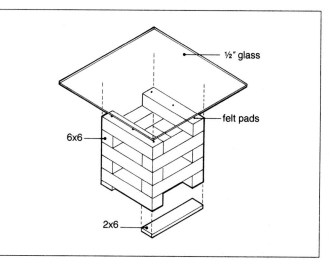

Setting up a timber table like the one shown *below* may be one of the most eye-catching, easy-to-assemble projects you'll ever make. With pieces precut by a lumberyard, you can build the table without tools—just sand, finish, and stack the timbers, topping them with a sheet of glass or acrylic. (For a coffee table, simply build it lower.)

To begin, buy 6x6 timbers cut to size, or cut them yourself. You need 20 feet of 6x6 wood, *accurately* cut into 2-foot pieces. Also, pick up two 2-foot pieces of 2x6s. Used as base runners, they raise the table to the common dining height of 29½ inches.

Sand each piece of wood, then stain and varnish, or apply two coats of polyurethane. After the wood dries, stack it as shown. Weight will stabilize the table, but if you want to ensure its stability, glue each piece as you stack.

To protect the ½-inch-thick polished, tempered glass top, glue thin, circular felt pads to the top of the wood. With an acrylic top, use rubber pads.

Finish the work by centering the sheet of glass or acrylic atop the wood. Its weight will also keep it in place.

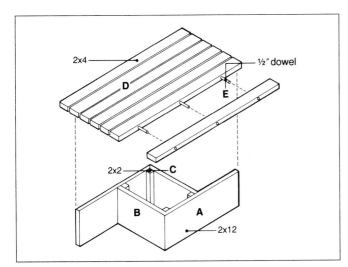

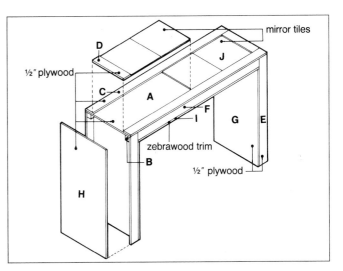

This 48x26x13-inch redwood table can be made any size you like, using redwood 2x12s, 2x4s, and 2x2s, four angle braces, ½-inch dowels, glue, varnish, screws, and stain.

First, build a boxy base from the 2x12s (A,B), installing butt joints that you glue and nail in place. Use 2x2 blocking strips (C) to reinforce the corners. Glue and nail these, also.

Next, make the top from the 2x4s (D). Drill three ½-inch holes through each piece of wood. Sand, stain, and varnish

the wood with three coats of varnish. Then sand, stain, and varnish the base.

Stain the dowels (E), push them through the holes in the top, and glue them in place. To form the tabletop, slide the 2x4s into position, gluing each one to the dowels and leaving some space between them. Sand, stain, and varnish the ends of the dowels.

To permanently attach the tabletop to the base, invert both pieces on the floor. Then screw the angle braces to the top and each corner 2x2.

This classy console table measures 54x18⅛x36 inches, but adjust the dimensions to suit yourself. You need ½-inch plywood, pine 2x2s, mirror tiles, ½-inch zebrawood trim, vinyl fabric, tile adhesive, white wood glue, screws, and nails.

First, cut the top panel (A) from the plywood. Attach 2x2 nailers (B), then frame the top with plywood strips butted together (C,D). They should overhang the edges ½ inch.

To form the legs, glue and screw 3-inch-wide plywood

verticals (E), one in each corner, to the 2x2s and to the top.

Cover the horizontal nailers on both sides with 3-inch-wide plywood strips (F). Glue and nail them in place. Then face the inside and outside of the table legs with panels (G,H).

Using white glue, cover the table with vinyl fabric; stretch it tight enough to remove the wrinkles. To finish the job, glue the zebrawood strips to each side of the table (I). Then apply tile adhesive, and press the mirror tiles (J) into place.

FURNITURE
BY THE
ROOMFUL

Make room for this set of furniture, and you'll have pieces that work together equally well in a living room, family room, or den.

On its own, the table is even more versatile (the one shown here measures 40½x34½ inches). Just flip the base, and it becomes either a 16-inch-high coffee table or a 30-inch-high dining table.

Build it any size you like. Start with ¾-, ½-, and ¼-inch birch plywood; 2x2s of fir or pine; and a ¼-inch glass top with polished edges, cut to fit.

First, make a pattern, and cut the tabletop shape from the ¾-inch plywood. Frame the outer edge with the ¼-inch plywood, then paint the top, trimming the edge with vinyl veneer.

Cut the 2x2s to size, and build the frame for the base, butting the wood together with glue and nails.

Next, cut pieces of the ½-inch plywood to face the inside of the 2x2 frame. Miter the plywood edges, and glue and nail them into place, insetting the nailheads and filling the holes. Similarly, face the outside of the frame with plywood pieces, mitered, glued, and nailed. Inset the nailheads, and fill all of the holes.

Miter the edges of 2½-inch-wide plywood strips. Glue and nail them into place around the base. Sink the nails.

To complete the table, paint the base, and set the glass into the frame. Cushion the glass with thin pieces of felt.

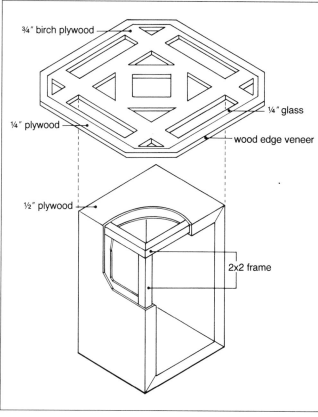

Diagram labels: ¾″ birch plywood · ¼″ glass · ¼″ plywood · wood edge veneer · ½″ plywood · 2x2 frame

To make the chair, use ¾-inch birch plywood, 1½-inch canvas strapping, and 1¼-inch dowels.

Cut the outsides of the chair and round the corners. Drill 1¼-inch holes ½ inch deep for the supporting dowels. Cut the dowels to fit, and glue and nail them into the holes on one side. Inset the nails, fill all of the holes and plywood edges, then paint the chair.

Cut strapping; rivet ends to form six loops. Slip the loops onto the dowels, running each around the back bottom dowel. Glue and nail the second side to the dowels.

Build the plant stand from ¾-inch plywood and dowels. First, cut six rings, three with a diameter of 12 inches on the outside, 10 inches on the inside, and three measuring 11½ inches on the outside, 10 inches on the inside. Glue one of each smaller ring to one larger ring. (You may omit the smaller rings.) Then cut eight dowels to the desired height.

Drill holes through the center ring and matching holes ½ inch deep in the top and bottom rings. Insert dowels, glue them in place, and paint.

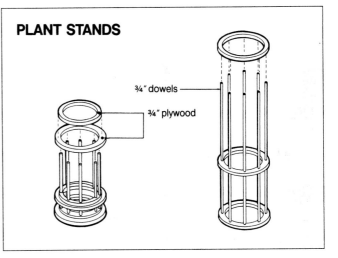

PLANT STANDS

¾" dowels

¾" plywood

To make the desk, you will need half-round split bamboo molding, ¾-inch birch plywood, and shelf brackets. Cut the top and front plates to size. Then cut two identical sides. Glue and screw the sides, top, and bottom, using butt joints. Set the screw heads flush. Trim the edges with the molding, then paint the desk. Position the desk top 29 inches from the floor. Using the shelf brackets, anchor the finished project to the studs.

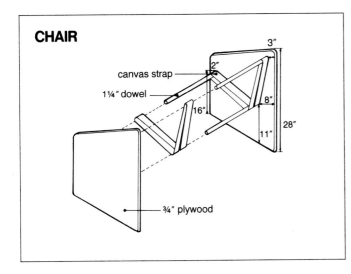

CHAIR

canvas strap

1¼" dowel

3"

2"

16"

8"

11"

28"

¾" plywood

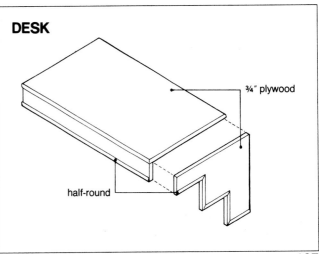

DESK

¾" plywood

half-round

FURNITURE BY THE ROOMFUL

(continued)

Don't let budget-biting prices prevent you from creating and enjoying an attractive, modern dining room. The modular pieces shown here are serviceable, sturdy, and inexpensive to build—and you can size them to fit the available space. (The dining table shown measures 48x24x30 inches; the seats are 19½x19½x16 inches; and the stacking tables measure 15x15x14¾ inches.)

To make the dining table, you need ¾-inch birch plywood and 1x4s of pine, fir, or birch. First, make a frame for the top from the 1x4s. Glue and nail together, countersink nailheads, and fill holes.

Cut a top from the plywood, fitting it to the frame, flush with the top edge of the 1x4s. Glue and nail together, countersink nailheads, and fill holes.

Cut out slotted table legs and glue them together, using edge cross-lap joints. If you like, fill the plywood edges, then paint the top and legs. When the paint dries, set the top on the legs and attach angle braces for extra support.

The seats also require ¾-inch plywood and 1x4s of pine, fir, or birch. Use the 1x4s to form the frame for the seat cushions. Miter the corners, glue, and nail. Cut out the plywood top, then glue and nail it to the frame.

Construct the leg assembly from notched plywood pieces. Screw the top to the legs, countersinking the screwheads. Finish the job by filling the exposed plywood edges and painting the seat.

Build the stacking tables with ¾-inch plywood, cutting the top from the wood. Then cut out slotted plywood legs and glue them together.

Glue and screw the top to the leg assembly. Fill the edges, and paint the tables.

DINING TABLE

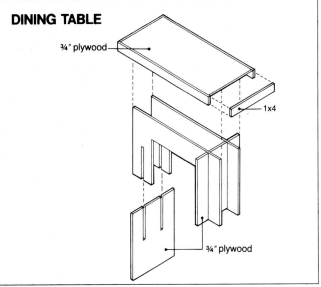

¾" plywood

1x4

¾" plywood

SEAT

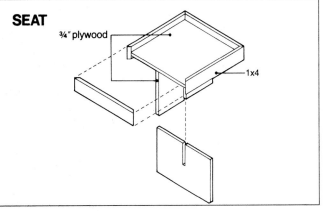

¾" plywood

1x4

STACKING TABLE

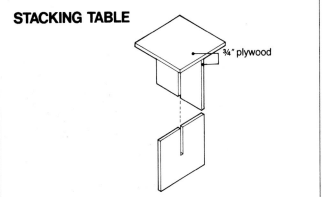

¾" plywood

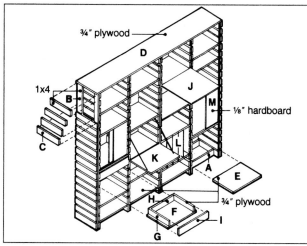

These shelves are made with 1/8-inch hardboard, 1x4s of pine or fir, 3/4-inch plywood, piano hinges, chain stops, and door tracks.

Sandwich each pair of uprights (B) between a series of 16-inch-long 1x4s (C). Space them 1 inch apart, keeping front and back edges flush; glue and nail to secure. Nail stretchers (A) between the bottom pairs of 1x4s to form a box with the front stretcher set back 3 inches. Glue and nail assembled sides to the boxes.

Cut plywood top (D) to size and nail it to the assembled sides. Stand unit upright and

place in position. Slide bottom shelves (E) in place. Dado the top of one shelf and bottom of another to receive hardboard vertical dividers (L). Apply strips of plastic bypassing door track on top and bottom of two shelves. Slip sliding doors (M) into tracks.

Screw a piano hinge to edge of shelves for closable sections. Screw doors (J,K) to piano hinges on the shelf. Use chain stops on door (K) to hold shelf level. Assemble the drawers (F,G,H,I). Extend the drawer bottom 3/4 inch beyond each side of drawer. Install drawers; sand and paint unit.

Sometimes, shelves have to measure up to big assignments. This divider —all 51x120x16 1/4 inches of it—is perfect for storing stereo components, records, and large books.

To build something similar, you need 3/4- and 1/4-inch plywood, 2x4s of pine or fir, glue, nails, wood filler, and paint. Before beginning, check the height of your ceiling, and size the divider to fit.

Cut the surround (A,C) and shelves (D) from 3/4-inch plywood. To fit shelves flush against verticals, cut grooves in the verticals deep and wide

enough to accept the shelf support strips. Fasten strips to the verticals 12 inches apart.

Position the five main pieces on the floor and assemble with butt joints, using glue and finishing nails. Glue and nail the plywood back (B) to each of the verticals and top and bottom. Cut 2x4s (E,F,G,H) to length. Cut H about 1/4 inch less than floor-to-ceiling height.

Sand and stain all 2x4s. Fasten E,F,G to the unit with screws from the inside. Position the unit in the room and attach outer 2x4 uprights (H). Seal and paint all the plywood. Varnish the 2x4s.

STORAGE UNITS

This handsome project is stylishly practical. Measuring 54 inches wide, 66 inches high, and 14 inches deep, it's a see-through divider that fits in anywhere.

You can make one like it by using ¾-inch plywood, 1x2s, 4x4s, glass doors, hardware, and sliding door tracks.

First, build the base in the shape of a five-sided box, with the two ends extending the full height of the unit. Next, install the vertical member and horizontal shelves inside the base. To make the top, build a four-sided box to fit between the ends. Then shape the 4x4s

into support pieces, as shown in the drawing, and screw them to the bottom.

Cut and install the flush doors, using knife hinges to attach them. Put up brackets for the glass shelf, and mount the track for the sliding doors near the edges of both sides of the cabinet.

Complete the work by cutting 1x2 trim and installing it in front of the tracks. Add a metal vertical bracket in the center for support. Finally, have the glass cut to size so the two pieces on each side overlap each other by 1 inch. (A dealer can grind the edges.)

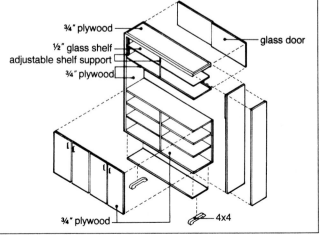

¾" plywood
½" glass shelf
adjustable shelf support
¾" plywood
glass door
¾" plywood
4x4

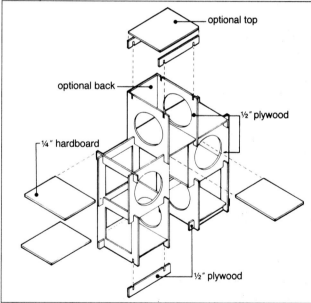

optional top

optional back

½″ plywood

¼″ hardboard

½″ plywood

S lotted panels allow you to assemble this unit in a number of ways. Start with ½-inch plywood, ¼-inch hardboard, wood tape or veneer, and paint or stain. In each top and bottom edge of ten 2-foot squares of ½-inch plywood, cut two 2-inch-deep, ½-inch-wide notches. The outside edge of each notch should be 3 inches from the corner of each piece. In the same way, notch eight horizontal braces on one edge.

On six squares, center 18-inch-diameter circles. On the other four squares, center 18-inch squares. Then cut out the inside shapes and sand. Apply wood tape or veneer to the exposed edges. Stain or paint both sides of the plywood. Paint the hardboard shelves.

STORAGE UNITS

(continued)

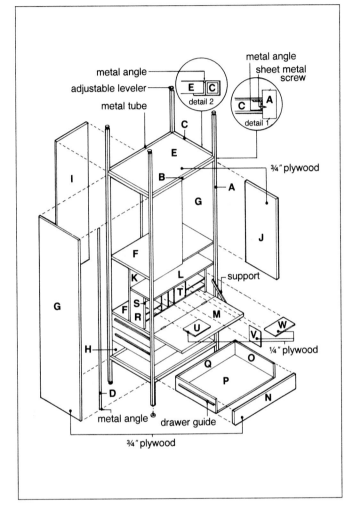

metal angle
adjustable leveler
metal tube

metal angle
sheet metal screw

detail 2

detail 1

¾″ plywood

support

¼″ plywood

metal angle   drawer guide

¾″ plywood

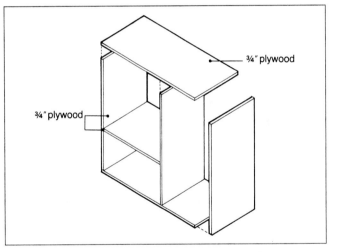

¾″ plywood

¾″ plywood

This practical storage project, *opposite,* makes a roomy desk as well as an efficient room divider. To begin, you will need ¾- and ¼-inch plywood, 1x1 metal tubing, a ⅝x⅝ metal angle, sheet metal screws, piano and pivot hinges, a leaf support, drawer guides, latches, plastic laminate and adhesive, nails, stain, and varnish.

Insert threaded adjustable legs into the metal tubes (A). Build the frame (A,B,C) to size, and stand it in place, making sure it's level. Position the top and bottom (E) on metal angles screwed to B,C. Screw

long metal angles (D) to the uprights (A), and secure the sides (G) to the angles.

Then rabbet the sides (O) and backs (Q) of the drawers for the bottoms (P) to fit in. Attach the fronts (N) and guides.

Nail the horizontals (F) and divider (K) in place; assemble the storage frame (L,R). Attach the support for the dividers (T,U,V,W), then attach the facer (S). Position the unit, and attach to the divider (K). Mount the guides, doors (I,J), and back (H). Cover the inside surface of the desk panel (M) with plastic laminate; hinge the panel (M) to the shelf (F). Finish.

These storage modules are simple to build and versatile enough to go anywhere in your house. They also work effectively when placed on any of their sides. The units shown here are 24 inches square and 11 inches deep, but you can build them to any size you like, using ¾-inch plywood.

Cut the sides to size, with 45-degree angles on the ends for miter joints. If the objects you plan to store are lightweight, butt joints will work equally well.

Cut dadoes in the sides for the inside divider shelves, and

dado the vertical shelf where it meets the horizontal shelf. Then assemble the sides with white glue and finishing nails, using corner clamps to hold them in place. Countersink the nails.

Measure, cut, and assemble the two shelves. Apply glue to the dadoes, slip the vertical member in place, and nail it. Then nail in the shorter horizontal shelf.

To complete the project, fill the nail holes, and apply wood veneer tape to the edges, or fill with water-base wood putty, and sand lightly. Enamel or paint the unit.

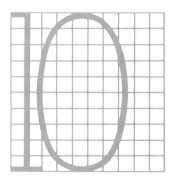

CLEANING & MAINTAINING YOUR FURNISHINGS

Total up what you've spent for all the sofas, draperies, tables, chairs, carpeting, and other furnishings in your family centers, and you'll probably discover that you're sitting on or near a substantial investment. Chapter 4—Choosing and Buying Furniture— tells how to build your furnishings portfolio. On the pages that follow you'll find advice on routine care, emergency measures, and cleaning tips for all your family center furnishings.

WOOD FURNITURE

Wood doesn't like extremes. Too much light or heat and too much humidity—or too little —can ruin a once-fine piece. Avoid placing wood furniture in front of a heat source, in direct sunlight, or in damp locations. If dry winter air is a problem at your house, a power humidifier can help prevent cracking and weakening of glued joints.

Most wood furniture pieces have a varnish, lacquer, or oil finish. All need to be dusted regularly with a clean, dry, lint-free cloth. Feather dusters don't pick up the dirt—they just relocate it. Oil- and polish-treated dust cloths work fine with oil finishes, but they can soften wax and gum up the surface on others.

Most wood finishes benefit from a regular cleaning to remove accumulated dirt and air-borne pollutants. You can use an emulsified oil cleaner/polish, soap and water, or furniture wash to do the job. Use only the suds of the cleaner, not the liquid itself. Dip a clean lint-free cloth in the suds and wring it out well before going over the finish. Rinse each small section at once with a second cloth that has been dipped in warm water and wrung out. Never let water stand on a wood finish. If the surface whitens, go over it with a soft cloth.

When the piece is thoroughly dry, finish with a commercial or a homemade polish (see recipe, *opposite page*). Rub with the grain until the gloss is restored. Then go over the whole piece with a cotton flannel polisher.

REMOVING STAINS

- *Water marks and rings.* Place clean, thick blotters over the stain and press with a warm iron; repeat. Or apply camphorated oil with a lint-free cloth; rub with the grain and wipe dry.
- *White marks.* Rub with a thin paste of wax and mineral spirits. When the paste dries, apply a thin coat of wax or polish. Or rub with cigar or cigarette ashes, using a cloth dipped in wax or salad oil. Wipe off at once. Rewax or polish.
- *Heat marks.* Rub gently— a tiny area at a time—with a dry steel-wool soap pad, then wipe up the powdery residue. Or rub with a cloth dampened in mineral spirits. Rub dry with a clean cloth; repeat.
- *Candle wax.* Harden with an ice cube; catch moisture as ice melts. Crumble off wax with your fingers, then scrape away the remainder. Rub with a cloth dampened in mineral spirits, then with liquid polish; wipe dry.
- *Milk or alcohol.* Use your fingers to rub paste wax or liquid into the area. Or rub in a paste of boiled linseed oil and rottenstone. Use powdered pumice for dull finishes. Wipe dry; polish.
- *Nail polish.* Rub the area gently with fine steel wool dipped in liquid wax. Wipe away the polish and rewax.
- *Paint spots.* If the paint is wet, treat it like a nail polish stain. If it's dry, soak the area with boiled linseed oil until the paint softens, then wipe away the paint with a cloth that has been dampened in linseed oil. If any paint remains, rub it away with a paste of boiled linseed oil and rottenstone.

CARING FOR WOOD FURNITURE

	REGULAR CLEANING	REMOVING SCRATCHES
HIGH GLOSS	Maintain finish with a liquid polish or paste wax applied as needed. Let liquid dry, then buff with a soft, lint-free cloth. Apply paste wax in a thin, even coat using a dry cloth; rub with the grain. Buff with a dry cloth while wax is still moist to bring out the sheen. Use a light-colored wax on blond or natural woods; use a dark one on mahogany or cherry. Even the lightest wax darkens in time.	Rub broken nutmeat (walnut, Brazil, or butternut) into the scratch, or touch up with furniture crayon or shoe polish in a matching shade. Rub the coloring agent only into the scratch to avoid discoloring the surrounding area.
SATIN GLOSS	Use a cleaning polish or a cream wax without silicone. Dust regularly with a soft lint-free cloth. Equal parts of raw linseed oil, turpentine, and vinegar make a good polish for fine woods. Apply a thin coat and use lots of muscle when polishing. If the finish is not well polished it becomes gummy and attracts dust, dirt, and grime.	Use aged or darkened iodine to fill scratches on mahogany or cherry wood. For maple, dilute the iodine 50/50 with denatured alcohol. Deep scratches call for professional filling and refinishing.
LOW GLOSS	Use a cleaning wax that removes surface soil and protects the finish without producing a shine, or a liquid polish specially designed for low-luster wood.	Nutmeats or boiled linseed oil may hide minor scratches. Avoid paste polishes, as they will create a noticeable shine on low-luster finishes.
OIL	Wash the surface occasionally with a mild soap solution to which a few drops of mineral spirits or lemon juice have been added. Rinse and dry the surface. Then, apply boiled linseed oil. Dust with a cloth dampened with water and glycerine or mineral thinner.	Use a fine steel-wool pad; rub lightweight mineral oil, boiled linseed oil, or paraffin oil into the scratch. Wipe dry.
ANTIQUE	Treat the same way as high-gloss finish wood furniture. Do not allow a heavy wax buildup. Paste wax preserves the patina and helps camouflage minor blemishes. If a piece has been refinished, follow recommendations for its new finish.	Do not attempt to repair scratches that paste wax won't cover up. The value of the antique can be destroyed. If a piece is severely damaged, consult a professional furniture restorer.

CASUAL
FURNITURE

CARING FOR CASUAL FURNITURE

	REGULAR CARE	SPOT/STAIN REMOVAL
PLASTIC	Wipe regularly with a damp cloth or a cloth dampened in a detergent/water solution. Blot dry with a soft, lint-free cloth or chamois.	Worn and spotted areas can be restored with a single-step auto cleaner/wax. Waxing can prevent future minor scratches.
WICKER	Use a vacuum cleaner with brush attachment to dust woven areas. Wipe regularly with a damp sponge or wash with a soapy sponge. Rinse well to remove all traces of cleaning agent. Wipe dry.	Use strong detergent solution to treat spots and stains; try in an inconspicuous place before using on visible surface.
RATTAN	Vacuum with a cleaner brush as with other types of wicker furniture.	Use sudsy ammonia/water or detergent/water solution for cleaning problem areas. Scrub dirty crevices with an old toothbrush. Rinse with clear water and dry thoroughly.
METAL	Dust regularly and clean with a mild detergent/water solution. Dry with a soft, lint-free cloth.	Spots and stains seldom permeate the finish. May require refinishing to remove rust. On wrought iron use steel wool and kerosene, if needed, to treat and remove rust spots.
PAINTED WOOD	Wipe to remove surface dust. Clean with mild detergent and water solution. Do not allow water to stand on paint. Dry thoroughly with a soft cloth.	Paint cleaners with mild abrasives will successfully remove some stains. Test in a small, inconspicuous area to make certain the cleaner does not remove the finish of gloss paint.
OIL FINISHES	Dust with a dampened cloth. Wash with a mild detergent solution; rinse and dry at once.	Use detergent solution with a few drops of lemon juice added to lighten stains. May require sanding and reoiling to restore unblemished surface.

SPECIAL TREATMENT

Do not use abrasive cleansers, furniture polish, or chemical cleaners. Wipe or rub with the length of the piece. Circular motions can cause permanent swirl marks.

Scrub wicker furniture of all types with a soft brush and gentle detergent solution. To prevent drying out, wipe at least once a year (or more often if needed) with a damp cloth. Dry thoroughly. If painted finish needs restoration, apply a glossy alkyd or latex paint. Renew shellac on unpainted wicker. Rub on liquid furniture wax for sheen and extra protection.

If the finish can tolerate water, treat to a shower in the tub or from the garden hose to prevent drying and splitting. Use towels to absorb excess moisture; allow to air-dry slowly out of direct sunlight.

Keep paint in good condition on non-rustproof metal. If refinishing is needed, first remove all traces of rust (any left will continue to spread), then coat with metal primer. Apply two or more coats of finish paint.

Use paste wax on darker sealed surface paints; creamy liquid wax on lighter ones. This makes the painted finish easier to care for and gives protection against spills and surface scratches.

Treat to a new coat of boiled linseed oil after cleaning. Apply with a lint-free, soft cloth and rub in thoroughly, working with the grain of the wood. Wipe up excess oil to avoid attracting dust to the surface.

As its name implies, most casual furniture can hold its own against kids, dogs, spills, and most of the wear and tear an active family can dish out. But no furniture is absolutely indestructible or totally maintenance-free, casual included. The chart *at left* summarizes casual's cleaning and care requirements. For additional guidance, consider these points.

• Plastic furniture loses its luster with wear and when it's subjected to harsh abrasive cleaners. It should be dusted regularly, but gently. Even dust can cause minute scratches that add up to a cloudy surface over a period of time. Use a damp cloth to dust and mop up spills. When fruit juices, ink, or rust has left a stain on a plastic surface, treat it first with a mild detergent and water bath. Rinse well and dry with a soft cloth. Then apply a one-step car cleaner wax. Rub with the length of the piece.

Don't be tempted to try a chemical cleaner or a spot remover on plastic—the results will be disastrous. Because some printed plastic surfaces wear off with use, you should protect them with coats of liquid wax. Reapply as needed to keep these surfaces looking top-notch.

• Acrylic surfaces (such as Plexiglas and Lucite) can be scratched extremely easily. Clean and dust them with an ammonia and water solution or mild detergent and water. Use the auto cleaner/wax that is recommended for most plastic furniture to retain a lustrous, scratch-resistant finish.

• Most glass surfaces usually require light but frequent care. To clean, use a commercial glass cleaner, or make your own from one tablespoon of ammonia or vinegar in a quart of water. Use lint-free cloths,

paper towels, or newspaper to dry the surface. Don't dust really dirty glass tops; clean them instead. Pushing the dirt particles around on the dry glass causes scratches.

• Wood furniture that has been "antiqued" with paint should be protected with wax. Use a paste wax for dark colors and a liquid wax for lighter ones. Either requires buffing. Waxing preserves the finish of the antiquing glaze.

• There are special furniture finishes that make wood harder, tougher, and more resistant to spills than normal. These "super finishes" are ideal for family room furniture because they stand up to rough treatment. Check labels when buying furniture to see if the piece you're considering has been treated with this special heat curing and sealing process. Super-finished pieces are cleaned and polished just like other fine wood furniture pieces. (For more information about furniture labels, see page 69.)

• True, unsealed lacquer finishes are rare and generally found on imported pieces. An unsealed piece is sensitive to solvent; if, for example, an alcoholic drink is spilled on a true lacquer finish, the surface is ruined. Most lacquer-type finishes manufactured in the United States are well sealed. Test the finish of your lacquer piece by using a cleaner in an inconspicuous spot. If no color rubs off, the cleaner you are using should be safe. Paste wax can be used after cleaning, as can spray-type furniture finishes. Dust any lacquer finish gently. A dry cloth can cause dirt particles to scratch the surface.

UPHOLSTERY

CARING FOR UPHOLSTERY

	REGULAR CARE	SPOT AND STAIN REMOVAL
COTTON	Vacuum regularly to remove ground-in dust and dirt. Turn cushions to distribute wear.	Soak up spills as they happen. Many stains are set by hot water and detergents. Sponge oily stains with cleaning fluid or a spray-on dry cleaner that absorbs grease. Use a blotter under stains if possible.
LINEN	Brush or vacuum regularly. Removing the surface dirt lengthens the time before an overall cleaning is needed and extends the life of the fabric.	Don't use a bleach solution to remove or lighten stains; bleach weakens the fibers and leaves its own stain. Use cool water and a small amount of upholstery cleaner foam on non-oily stains; use cleaning fluid or spray on oily stains. An absorbent towel or blotter under the fabric soaks up moisture before it reaches the cushion filling.
WOOL	Pet hairs cling to wool and vacuuming won't budge them. Use a natural-bristle brush or a lint remover before giving the whole piece a vacuum cleaning.	Sponge stain with cool water. If necessary, work a small amount of foam upholstery cleaner into the area. Rinse well with a clean cloth dipped in warm water and wrung dry.
LEATHER	Brush suede with a fine bristle brush to remove soil and dust. Dust smooth leather regularly and wipe down with a mild leather soap and water solution. Rinse off soap residue and buff dry with a soft untreated cloth.	Clean headrests and other soil-prone areas often to prevent oily buildup. Test commercial cleaners in a hidden spot before using overall. Leather or suede that is very discolored will require professional cleaning.
NYLON & ACRYLIC	Require only regular vacuuming to remove surface dust and soil.	Treat stains at once. Water-based stains are easily removed with foam upholstery cleaner. Oil-based stains require immediate treatment with upholstery cleaner or cleaning fluid. These stains will set if not taken out at once.
SYNTHETIC LEATHER	Dust to remove surface soil. Clean with a cloth dipped in warm water and mild detergent. Rub briskly with a soft cloth. Wipe with a water-dampened cloth to remove cleaner residue.	Remove ball-point pen marks with alcohol; rinse with clear water. Cleaning fluid works well on most other stains. Apply paste wax to areas that are subject to staining. Buff well.

SPECIAL TREATMENT

Soil-repellent finishes make cotton an easy upholstery fabric to live with. Untreated cotton absorbs moisture readily and takes longer to dry than man-made fibers.

Before cleaning, make sure your upholstery can take it. Test a small inconspicuous area with foam cleaner and allow it to dry before tackling the whole chair or sofa.

After cleaning, dry furniture as quickly as possible with windows open. Don't subject it to artificial heat or direct sunlight. Make certain fabric has been treated with a moth repellent; repeat as often as necessary.

Do not use a surface-protecting spray on suede or leather. To avoid cracking, keep piece out of direct sunlight. High humidity can cause mildew.

These fibers have excellent resistance to soil, abrasion, and moisture. Both clean well with commerical products and dry rapidly.

Keep synthetic leathers away from direct sun and other heat sources. High humidity can cause mildew on vinyl surfaces.

Dust is upholstery's hidden enemy. Just because you can't see it doesn't mean that dirt isn't lurking in fabrics and wearing them out from the inside. Eventually dirt particles cut through even the toughest upholstery fibers and shorten their lives.

A weekly vacuuming is the cheapest upholstery insurance policy you can buy. Use the appropriate attachments to get down into corners and crevices. A good, stiff brush helps clean around seams, tufts, and welting. After you finish, turn the cushions to distribute wear on fabric and stuffing material.

Feather-filled cushions shouldn't be vacuumed; the suction will pull the ends of the feathers through the fabric. Use a stiff brush to remove dust. Fluff the cushions and air them outside as needed.

Cleaning strategies

Remove spills and spots on all fabrics as soon as possible. Use the chart *at left* as a guide for spot and spill removal. Quick action can often save a piece of fabric from becoming permanently stained.

When a general cleaning is called for, check the fiber content of your fabric first before proceeding. Leave pile fabrics such as corduroy, velvet, and plush to professional cleaners. Most other fabrics can be cleaned quite well with home methods. You can use a commercial foam cleaner or your own homemade formula. Never use soap on upholstered furniture because it can't be rinsed off well and the remaining soap residue attracts soil like a magnet. Test the fabric in an inconspicuous place to be sure it will safely react to the cleaner you've chosen.

You can make a dry foam using mild detergent and warm water. Whip the solution until you have lots of foam. It's the lather you want for the job, not the liquid. The fabric must absorb as little moisture as possible; otherwise it will mildew before it dries. Use a soft-bristle brush or a sponge to apply the foam. Work quickly, scrubbing with a circular motion. Lift off the dirty suds with a rubber spatula, dry sponge, or clean towel. Rinse the area with a clean cloth dipped in warm water and wrung almost dry. Work in small areas until the entire surface has been cleaned.

Dry furniture as quickly as you can; open the windows or set electric fans to blow on the fabric. Don't put the furniture in direct sunlight, however—you risk fading the fabric. Let the fabric get bone-dry before you use it again.

Spray-on fabric protectors retard fading, staining, and soil, and sometimes repel liquids. These finishes make the fabric easier to clean, but they don't make it wear longer. If your fabric has been treated with one of these sprays, be sure to consult the manufacturer's directions before cleaning. After a piece is completely dry, several light coats of a soil-retardant spray will keep the cleaning job looking fresh.

CARPET & DRAPERIES

The carpet on your floor represents a considerable investment—one that will give you a good return for many years, if you keep your carpet in top-notch condition.

Aside from regular vacuuming, give your carpet a thorough vacuuming—that means five to seven times over the *same area*—at least every few weeks. This deep cleaning removes ground-in dirt that causes fibers to wear quickly.

Once or twice a year you'll need to give your carpet a shampoo. This can be done by a professional carpet cleaner, or you can do it yourself with the aid of rental equipment and commercial cleaning products.

Wet or dry cleaning?
There are two basic types of carpet shampoos—wet and dry. In the wet method, a foam shampoo is applied by a hand brush, sponge mop, or electric rug shampooer. The residue is either removed with an extractor (in the case of most electric shampooers) or by vacuuming when the carpet is dry. In the dry method, an absorbent material is spread evenly with a stiff brush over a carpet that has been well vacuumed. The material absorbs oils and dirt, then it's vacuumed up.

Both methods have their place. The overall wet shampoo cleans deeply; but overwetting the carpet can cause shrinking and discoloration, and may not remove all the soap residue. If the cleaner is left in the carpet fiber, your carpet will get dirtier faster.

The dry method is ideal for quick pickups between deep cleanings. Usually only the surface dirt and oils are removed. Use the powdered cleaners with care on darker colored carpets; the powders are sometimes hard to vacuum up

and will show on deep-toned backgrounds.

Use a machine when cleaning a large area—the results are better and it's easier on you. Test any cleaner in a hidden spot or on a carpet scrap before starting on the whole rug. Not all fibers react well to all cleaning products.

You'll find it easier to clean wall-to-wall carpet if you remove all furniture from the room. Pretreat stains according to the methods recommended by the manufacturer of your selected cleaning agent. If you must move furniture back into the room before the carpet is bone dry, slip foil-backed cardboard squares under the casters, glides, and feet of all pieces to prevent rust stains and permanent marks. When the carpet is thoroughly dry, vacuum it well to remove any traces of the cleaning agent.

Maintaining carpet
Keep any carpeted room well aired. Stale, damp air promotes the growth of mildew, which can ruin carpets. If you do find a spot of mildew, brush and vacuum it well and sponge with a solution of mild detergent and water. Wall-to-wall carpet requires professional treatment when mildew develops.

Most carpets shed a bit. Vacuuming picks up these extra bits of fiber that are left in during manufacturing. Use a sharp pair of scissors to trim tufts even with the rest of the pile surface.

If your carpet seems to be filled with static electricity, you need to raise the humidity in the room or apply an anti-static spray finish to the fibers. Adding a humidifier or other water source works better; spray products generally act like dirt-catchers on the carpet surface.

CLEANING WINDOW COVERINGS

Clean and fresh-looking window coverings show off your windows to their best advantage. As with other furnishings, a little routine dusting and polishing stretches the time between heavy scrubbings.

Draperies
Any kind of fabric window treatment can benefit from regular dusting. Use the upholstery attachment of your vacuum cleaner or a good clothes brush to remove household dust. Start at the top and work down. Some unlined draperies lose dust with a brief tumble in the clothes dryer on a no-heat setting. Any thorough and regular dusting will stretch the time between all-over cleanings.

Generally, lined draperies are best sent out for cleaning by reliable professional dry cleaners. They have the equipment and the know-how, and for a fee they'll pick up the draperies and rehang them after cleaning. Be ready to tell the cleaners the fiber content of your window coverings.

Unlined draperies can be machine washed and dried if the material can take it. If your window coverings are large, consider using the commercial equipment at a coin-operated laundry instead of your own washing machine. The large-load machines minimize touch-up pressing on most wash-and-hang draperies.

Blinds
Horizontal and vertical blinds need regular dusting to look their best. Extend either type to its full length and clean both sides of each slat with a lint-free cloth or the dusting brush attachment of the vacuum.

Painted and plastic blinds can be cleaned with mild detergent-and-water suds when they're grimy. Use a cloth dipped in the suds that's been well wrung out and wash one slat at a time. Rinse and dry with a soft cloth.

The tape and cord on blinds can be washed and dried when they're soiled. If tapes and cords are beyond salvation, they can be replaced. Although it's a tedious job, you can do it yourself—or take the blinds to a window-covering dealer for repair.

Natural wood blinds and shutters are usually cleaned with a liquid type wax and buffed with a soft cloth.

Shades
Washable roller shades need to be taken down and cleaned on a flat surface. Use a mild detergent and water solution to make suds for scrubbing. Use a soft brush and work in small sections. Avoid getting the surface too wet. Rinse with a well-wrung-out damp cloth. When clean, hang without rerolling to dry. Non-washable shades can be cleaned with an art gum eraser or a commercial shade cleaner.

CARING FOR CARPET

	REGULAR CARE	SPOT/STAIN REMOVAL
WOOL	Vacuum regularly. Pilling and shedding are normal when carpet is new. Wool should be treated for insect-repellency every three to four years. Wool resists soil naturally but is harder to clean than man-made fibers. Wool absorbs moisture; during high-humidity periods, you should air carpeted rooms often.	Treat spots carefully. Always test remedies on a scrap or in an inconspicuous spot. Fibers are damaged by salt, full-strength ammonia, chlorine bleach, and strong detergents. Before resorting to stronger remedies, try plain water on fresh stains. Blot up excess water. If a special cleaning solution is needed for spot removal, apply with a medicine dropper and rinse thoroughly.
ACRYLIC	Areas of heavy traffic may require daily vacuuming to remove dirt. Acrylic greatly resists soil because dirt has less tendency to cling to smooth fibers. Acrylic fibers may tend to pill; there's no solution to this problem.	These fibers take well to home cleaning and spot-removal methods. Although they resist most stains, some oily substances may leave marks unless they are treated with a foam cleaning agent or cleaning solvent. Wipe and pat pile gently rather than scrubbing.
NYLON	These fibers are sneaky—they hide dirt so well that you think they don't need much care, but you should vacuum thoroughly at least once a week. Nylon has a tendency to build up static electricity; make certain you have adequate humidity in the area or use an antistatic spray on the carpet.	Very resistant to soil stains, most acids, and solvents. Spot-clean with water first before switching to a cleaning solution.
POLYESTER	Pick up daily accumulation of dust and lint with a carpet sweeper. Vacuum thoroughly at least once a week. Polyester resists most soiling and cleans well.	Use a spray carpet cleaner for water-soluble stains, a dry-cleaning solvent on oil-based ones. Use a small amount of either cleaner, and blot liquid; continue working until no more of the stain can be removed.
POLYPRO-PYLENE	Easy to care for; less prone to static cling than others, so dirt has little to stick to. Does not mat down even in heavy traffic areas. Fibers are not harmed by moisture. Vacuum regularly to remove dirt.	This strong fiber is the most stain-resistant of all. It resists almost all acids and chemicals. Mop up spills as they occur. Treat oil-based spots with dry-cleaning solvent. Blot until no more of the stain can be removed. Use detergent solution on water-soluble spills.

WHERE TO GO FOR MORE INFORMATION

Better Homes and Gardens® Books
Want to learn more about decorating, remodeling, or maintaining your family centers? These Better Homes and Gardens® books can help.

Better Homes and Gardens®
NEW DECORATING BOOK
How to translate ideas into workable solutions for every room in your home. Choosing a style; furniture arrangements; windows, walls, and ceilings; floors; lighting; and accessories. 433 color photos, 76 how-to illustrations, 432 pages.

Better Homes and Gardens®
COMPLETE GUIDE TO HOME REPAIR,
MAINTENANCE, & IMPROVEMENT
Inside your home, outside your home, your home's systems, basics you should know. Anatomy and step-by-step drawings illustrate components, tools, techniques, and finishes. 515 how-to techniques; 75 charts; 2,734 illustrations; 552 pages.

Better Homes and Gardens®
STEP-BY-STEP
CABINETS AND SHELVES
Materials and hardware, planning guidelines, the ABCs of cabinet construction, cutting and joining techniques, project potpourri. 155 illustrations, 96 pages.

Better Homes and Gardens®
STEP-BY-STEP
BASIC PLUMBING
Getting to know your system, solving plumbing problems, making plumbing improvements, plumbing basics and procedures. 42 projects, 200 illustrations, 96 pages.

Better Homes and Gardens®
STEP-BY-STEP
BASIC WIRING
Getting to know your system, solving electrical problems, making electrical improvements, electrical basics and procedures. 22 projects, 286 illustrations, 96 pages.

Better Homes and Gardens®
STEP-BY-STEP
BASIC CARPENTRY
Setting up shop, choosing tools and building materials, mastering construction techniques, building boxes, hanging shelves, framing walls, installing drywall and paneling. 10 projects, 191 illustrations, 96 pages.

Better Homes and Gardens®
STEP-BY-STEP
MASONRY & CONCRETE
Choosing tools and materials; planning masonry projects; working with concrete; working with brick, block, and stone; special-effect projects. 10 projects, 200 drawings, 96 pages.

Better Homes and Gardens®
STEP-BY-STEP
HOUSEHOLD REPAIRS
Basic tools for repair jobs, repairing walls and ceilings, floors and stairs, windows, doors, electrical and plumbing items. 200 illustrations, 96 pages.

Other Sources of Information
Most professional associations publish lists of their members and will be happy to send you their booklets upon request. They may also offer informational and educational material for the asking.

American Gas Association
1515 Wilson Blvd.
Arlington, VA 22209

American Hardboard Association (AHA)
887-B Wilmette Road
Palatine, IL 60067

American Home Lighting Institute
230 N. Michigan Avenue
Chicago, IL 60601

National Kitchen and Bath Association (NKBA)
114 Main Street
Hackettstown, NJ 07840

Association of Home Appliance Manufacturers (AHAM)
20 N. Wacker Drive
Chicago, IL 60606

Cellulose Manufacturers Association (CMA)
5908 Columbia Pike
Baileys Crossroads, VA 22041

Exterior Insulation Manufacturers Association (EIMA)
1000 Vermont Avenue NW, Suite 1200
Washington, DC 20005

Major Appliance Consumer Action Panel (MACAP)
20 N. Wacker Dr.
Chicago, IL 60606

National Association of the Remodeling Industry (NARI)
11 E. 44th St.
New York, NY 10017

National Housewares Manufacturers Association (NHMA)
1130 Merchandise Mart
Chicago, IL 60654

Tile Council of America
Box 326
Princeton, NJ 08540

ACKNOWLEDGMENTS

Architects and Designers
The following is a list by page number of the architects, project designers, and interior designers whose work appears in this book.

Page 7
Designer: Adelaide Osborne/Cybele Interiors. Builder: Ted Haggett
Pages 10-11
Designer: Barbara Palmer
Pages 12-13
Architect: Sheldon Hill
Pages 18-19
Designer: Woody Gruber
Pages 22-23
Architect: David Durrant
Pages 24-25
Designer: Suzie Emerson
Pages 28-29
Designer: Molly Epstein
Page 30
Architect: Tom Eldredge
Page 31
Architect: Jerry D. Nelson, Principal, AIA, Pomnitz/ Nelson Architects, P.C.
Page 32
Designer: Jon Bruton, Michele Olson
Page 33
Designers: Mr. and Mrs. Roger Simpson
Pages 34-35
Designer: Larry Deutsch, ASID
Page 37
Architect: Alan Meyers

Page 39
Architect: Robert Braunschweiger
Pages 40-41
Designer: Rita Little
Page 42
Architect: Robert I. Kaplan
Page 43
Architect: Chris Nicholson
Pages 46-47
Designer: Karen Marcus of Halls Crown Center
Page 48
Architect: Steve Wisenbaker
Page 49
Designer: Steve Habiague
Pages 50-51
Designers: Harry and Joyce Niewoehner
Pages 52-53
Designer: Gayle Jolluck, Ltd.
Pages 54-55
Designer: D. Dahken Interiors
Page 56
Architect: Richard M. Selleg
Page 60
Architect: Lawrence Horowitz
Page 61
Designer: Neil Frankel, Milton M. Schwartz and Assoc.
Pages 100-101
Designer: Sophia Marcovitz
Page 103
(Top) Architect: Finegold and Bullis. (Bottom) Architect: Michael L. Loia. Designer: Stan Topol/Devidts
Pages 104-105
J. Joseph
Pages 106-107
Architects: Rudi/Lee/Dreyer
Page 108
Architect: Erling Falck
Page 109
Designer: Jon Cockrell
Page 110
Designer: Barbara Palmer

Page 111
Architects: Fisher-Friedman Association. Designer: Louisa Cowan
Page 115
Designer: Suzy Taylor, ASID. Designer: Karen Novick
Page 118
Designer: Lloyd F. Barling
Page 119
Designer: Tony Torrice
Page 126
Designer: Kathleen Koszyk

Photographers and Illustrators
We extend our thanks to the following photographers and illustrators whose creative talents and technical skills contributed much to this book.

Ross Chapple
Richard Fish
George de Gennaro
Harry Hartman
Robert Hawks
Hedrich-Blessing
Thomas E. Hooper
William N. Hopkins and Associates
Fred Lyon
Maris/Semel
Bradley Olman
Ozzie Sweet
Jessie Walker

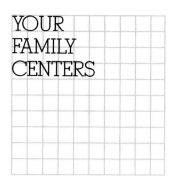
SELECTING SHEET GOODS

If you decide to construct one of the projects shown in Chapters 5, 6, or 9, you'll probably decide to use sheet goods. These man-made materials—typically 4x8-foot panels—come in a variety of forms, as shown *opposite*. All are highly resistant to warping, strong, easy to work with, and widely available.

• *Plywood.* To make plywood, manufacturers laminate thin layers (called plies) of wood to each other, using water-resistant glue for most *interior* types and waterproof adhesives for *exterior* plywoods. The front and back surface plies may be either softwood, usually Douglas fir, or any of several hardwood species.

• *Particleboard* and *hardboard* consist of wood particles, sawdust, and glue that have been compressed and bonded together by heat into a product that's dense, heavy, and durable. Some particleboard has a wood veneer surface.

• *Drywall* is nothing more than gypsum powder sandwiched between layers of very heavy paper. Applied to walls and ceilings, it's widely used as an interior surface material.

Smart buymanship begins with a knowledge of what's available. The chart below lists the sheet goods you'll find at most lumberyards and building material home centers, and the typical uses of each.

Sheet Goods Selector

Material	Grades and Common Types	Thickness (in inches)	Common Panel Sizes (in feet)	Typical Uses
Plywood	Softwood plywood A-A; A-B; A-C; A-D	¼; ⅜; ½; ½; ⅝; ¾	2x4; 4x4; 4x8	Projects in which appearance of one or both sides matters—cabinets, drawer fronts, bookcases, soffits, built-ins, shelves.
	C-D; CDX	⅜; ½; ¾	4x8	Sheathing; subflooring; underlayment.
	MDO (medium-density overlay)	⅜; ¾	4x8	Projects requiring an extra-smooth painting surface—tabletops, cabinets, outdoor signs.
	303 siding	⅜; ⅝; ¾	4x7; 4x8; 4x9	Exterior siding (smooth, grooved, reverse board-and-batten, and other textures); decorative wall and ceiling treatments.
	Hardwood plywood A-2 (good both sides) G1S (good one side)	¼; ¾ ¼	2x4; 4x8 4x8	Fine furniture and cabinetmaking; decorative wall panels.
Particle-board		⅜; ½; ⅝; ¾;	2x4; 4x4; 4x8	Underlayment; core material for laminated furniture and counter tops; speaker enclosures; closet lining (aromatic cedar particleboard).
Hardboard	Standard; Tempered (moisture-resistant)	⅛; ¼	2x4; 4x4; 4x8	Underlayment; drawer bottoms and partitions; cabinet backs; pegboard (*perforated hardboard*) decorative wall panels (prefinished hardboard).
Drywall	Regular; Moisture-resistant (MR); Fire-resistant (FR)	⅜; ½; ⅝	4x8; 4x12	Finish material for interior walls and ceilings; kitchen, bath, and basement surfaces (MR); surfaces in attached garages (FR); patch material for lath-and-plaster walls.

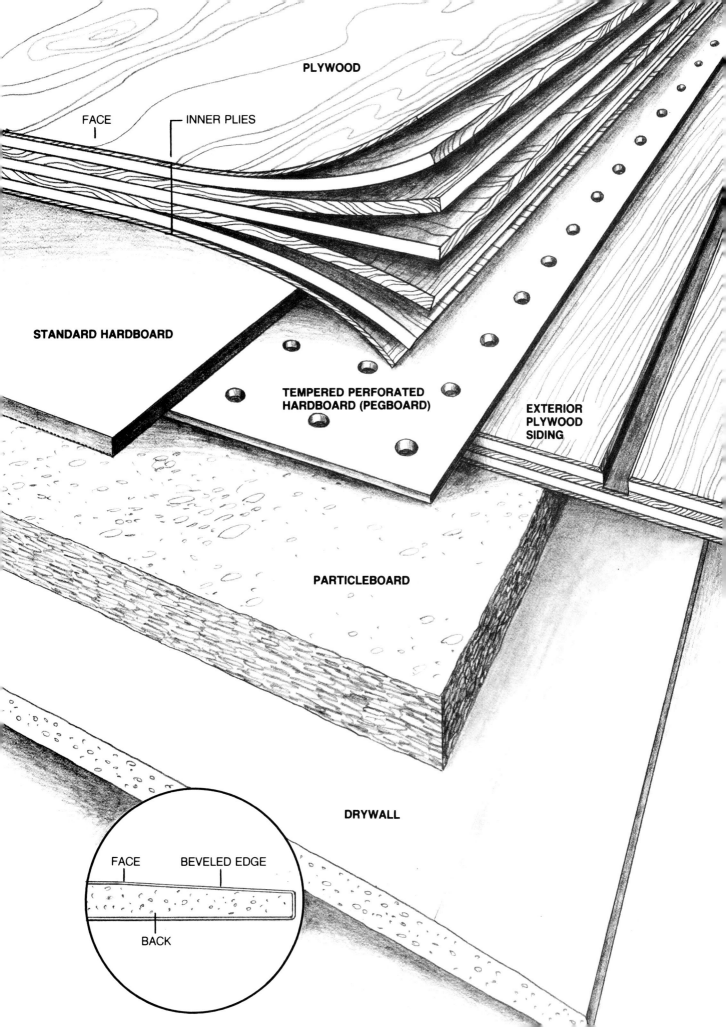

PLYWOOD

FACE

INNER PLIES

STANDARD HARDBOARD

TEMPERED PERFORATED
HARDBOARD (PEGBOARD)

EXTERIOR
PLYWOOD
SIDING

PARTICLEBOARD

DRYWALL

FACE BEVELED EDGE

BACK

SELECTING LUMBER

As a home carpenter, you will be buying lumber for various projects. Although you needn't become a lumber expert, you will need to know what's available, when to use what type and size lumber, and how to order this basic building material.

Lumber is available in two basic types—*softwoods* and *hardwoods*—each governed by different grading systems. The nature of your project determines to a large extent which type and grade to use.

• *Softwood* lumber—the type you'll use for most around-the-house projects—comes in two overall grade classifications: *select* and *common*. Use select lumber (B and Better, C,

and D) for any showy projects, such as cabinetry, where appearance is a vital consideration. For all other projects, common lumber (Nos. 1, 2, 3, and 4) will do well. The better the grade, the fewer defects there will be, and the more money you'll pay.

• *Hardwood* costs more than softwood, and is more difficult to work with; reserve it for very special furniture and trim. Hardwood grading is based primarily on the amount of clear surface area on the board. Heading the list is *FAS Grade* (Firsts and Seconds), which is the most knot-free grade, followed by *Select Grade, No. 1 Common,* and *No. 2 Common.*

Finally, keep in mind that both hardwood and softwood have a set of *nominal* dimensions (what you use for ordering purposes) and a set of *actual* dimensions (what you get after the lumber is milled and dried). A 2x4, for example, actually measures 1½ by 3½ inches.

Take a look at the chart *opposite.* It classifies lumber into five groupings, then lists common uses for each, as well as nominal and actual dimensions of various-size members.

Because of the array of lumber thicknesses and widths, lumberyard and home center personnel use the *board foot* to measure and price the amount of wood in a given

piece. (As shown *below left,* a board foot is defined as the wood equivalent to a piece 12 inches square and 1 inch thick.) Specify a piece's length in linear feet and the lumberyard will compute the cost.

When lumber shopping, be prepared with a list detailing your needs. To order, state the quantity, thickness, width, length, grade, and species —in that order. (For example: four 2x4 x 8-foot No. 2 fir.) After placing your order at the desk, walk out into the yard to see firsthand the lumber that you're getting. If you spot any of the defects shown *below right,* and if they'll seriously interfere with your use for the lumber, ask for replacements.

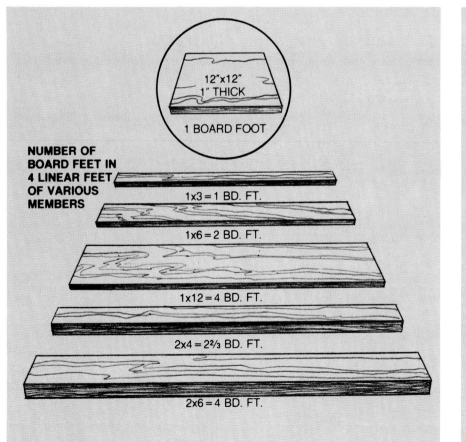

1 BOARD FOOT
12"x12"
1" THICK

NUMBER OF BOARD FEET IN 4 LINEAR FEET OF VARIOUS MEMBERS

1x3 = 1 BD. FT.
1x6 = 2 BD. FT.
1x12 = 4 BD. FT.
2x4 = 2⅔ BD. FT.
2x6 = 4 BD. FT.

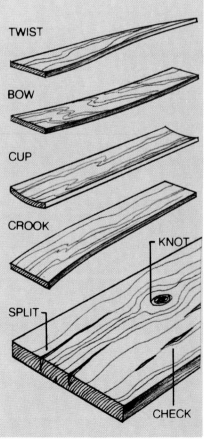

TWIST
BOW
CUP
CROOK
KNOT
SPLIT
CHECK

Type		Common Uses	Nominal Sizes	Actual Sizes
Strips		Furring for wall-paneling material (drywall, hardboard, plywood) and ceiling material (drywall, composition tiles); shims; spacers; blocking; bridging; stakes; forms; crates; light-duty frames; edging; latticework.	1x2 1x3	¾x1½ ¾x2½
Finish Lumber: Boards	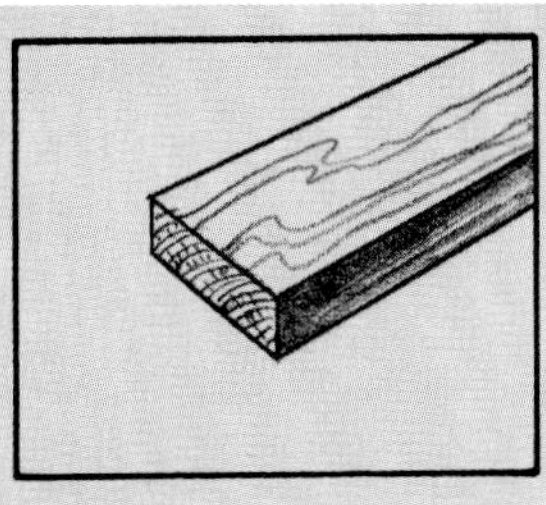	Interior paneling; exterior sheathing; structural framing and finishing; exterior siding and soffits; subflooring and flooring; decking; fencing; walks; interior and exterior trim; fascias; casing; valances; shelving; cabinets; closet lining; furniture; built-ins.	1x4 1x6 1x8 1x10 1x12	¾x3½ ¾x5½ ¾x7¼ ¾x9¼ ¾x11¼
Tongue and Groove	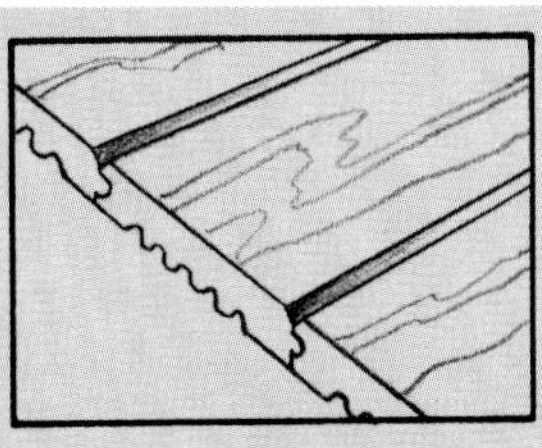	Subflooring; flooring; exterior sheathing and siding; decorative interior wall treatments.	1x4 1x6 1x8 1x10 1x12	Actual sizes vary from mill to mill.
Shiplap		Exterior sheathing and siding, decking; underlayment; subflooring; roof sheathing; decorative interior wall treatments.	1x4 1x6 1x8	¾x3⅛ ¾x5⅛ ¾x6⅞
Dimension Lumber		Structural framing (wall studs, ceiling and floor joists, rafters, headers, top and sole plates); structural finishing; forming; exterior decking and fencing; walks; benches; screeds, stair components (stringers, steps); boxed columns.	2x2 2x3 2x4 2x6 2x8 2x10 2x12	1½x1½ 1½x2½ 1½x3½ 1½x5½ 1½x7¼ 1½x9¼ 1½x11¼
Posts	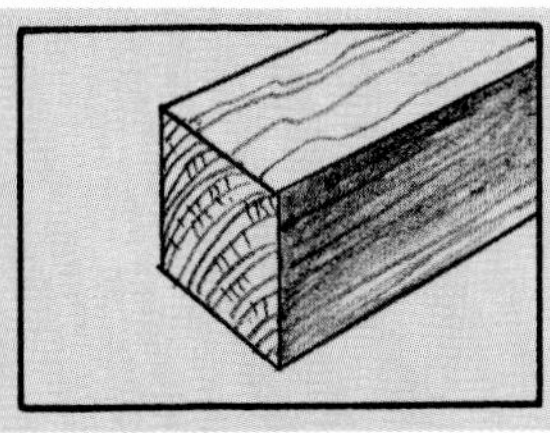	Heavy-duty structural framing; support columns; fencing; decking; turning material for wood lathes; building material for architectural and decorative interest.	4x4 6x6	3½x3½ 5½x5½
Timbers	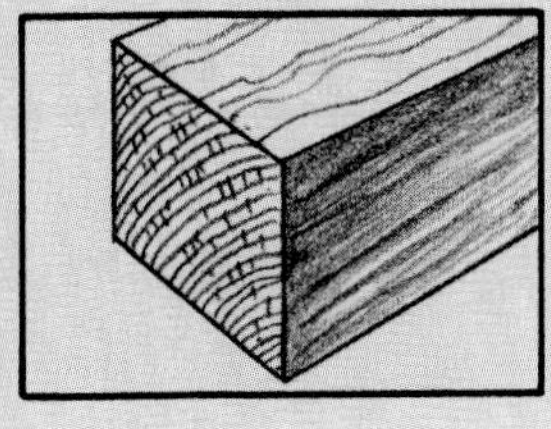	Heavy-duty structural framing; support columns; building material for architectural and decorative interest.	Rough-sawn; sizes vary.	Actual sizes vary slightly up or down from nominal sizes.

INDEX

(continued)